THE OTTOMAN TURKS

THE OTTOMAN TURKS

CANON EDWARD SELL

GYAN

Published by

Gyan Publishing House
5, Ansari Road
Daryaganj, New Delhi-110002
Phone: 011-47034999, 9811692060
E-mail: books@gyanbooks.com

Distribution Network
gyanbooks.com
India, USA, Canada, UK, Australia

ISBN: 978-93-7169-373-8 (PB)

First Published, 1915

2nd Impression 2025

Printed at: Gyan Press, Delhi.

THE OTTOMAN TURKS
Author: CANON EDWARD SELL

THE OTTOMAN TURKS

THE OTTOMAN TURKS

BY

THE REV. CANON SELL, D.D., M.R.A.S.

FELLOW OF THE UNIVERSITY OF MADRAS

AUTHOR OF 'THE FAITH OF ISLAM', 'THE RECENSIONS OF THE QUR'AN', 'THE RELIGIOUS ORDERS OF ISLAM', 'THE HISTORICAL DEVELOPMENT OF THE QUR'AN', 'THE LIFE OF MUHAMMAD', 'THE CULT OF 'ALI', 'MUSLIM CONQUESTS IN SPAIN', ETC.

1915

CONTENTS

THE OTTOMAN TURKS

I. THE RISE OF THE EMPIRE

AMONGST the numerous nomad races of Central Asia there were two great tribes—the Mongols and the Turks—who in the thirteenth century overran a great part of the Muslim empire and penetrated beyond it. Húlágú Khán captured Baghdad, the seat of the renowned 'Abbásid Khalífate, and the Mongols soon overran the Syrian empire of Saladin, which had come now under the rule of the Mamlúk Sulṭáns of Egypt. The Mongols on different occasions made several ineffectual attempts to invade Egypt, and were repulsed by the bravery of the Mamlúks;[1] but they entered Europe and advanced as far as Hungary. They were nomads and, as a rule, could not settle down; so after ravaging a country they usually retired from it. For a time, however, they retained possessions in China, and, as the Golden Horde, ruled in the Crimea; but they left no permanent mark on the Muslim empire of the Khalífate; and so we may pass them by.

[1] See *The Mamlúks in Egypt* (C.L.S.), pp. 10, 17, 21, 31.

The other branch of these great nomad barbarians, the Turks, did otherwise. They supplied the Khalífas of Baghdad with mercenary troops who soon became the rulers of their nominal masters. As imported slaves they attained also to royal power in Egypt. They founded a dynasty at Ghazni and captured Khurásán where they created the empire of the Seljúk Turks. Then came the great Mongol invasion under Chengiz Khán driving the Turks further south and west. Their clans under the names of the White and Black Weir (sheep) exercised much influence in the thirteenth century.

The Muslim empire at that time had almost passed away from its old Arab rulers. The Mongols had subdued Persia and advanced to the regions of the Volga and the Ural mountains, whilst Turks ruled in Asia Minor and Turkish Mamlúks held Egypt. Against these two Turkish powers the Mongols could do nothing. The Seljúk Sulṭáns of Iconium and the Mamlúks of Egypt held their own and remained when all fear of the Mongols had passed away. Amongst the tribes which followed the Seljúks was one which was led by its chief Ertoghul. It so happened that one day Ertoghul was proceeding with a small band of men in the direction of Anatolia, where he unexpectedly came upon a battlefield (Angora) in which the Seljúk Sulṭán was contending against a strong and determined foe. At once Ertoghul and his four hundred men joined in the conflict and helped to gain a victory for the Seljúks. On another occasion also they rendered valuable military assistance. The Sulṭán in return for this welcome aid allowed them to settle on land where good pasturage and suitable winter quarters were found. This was in the neighbourhood of Angora and not far from the boundaries of the Byzantine province of Bithynia.

In 1258, the year in which Baghdad fell, 'Uth-mán, the son of Ertoghul, was born. In due course he asserted his absolute independence, and founded the dynasty of the 'Uthmánulís, or as they are better known, the Ottoman Turks. With them our history begins. Thirty-five Sulṭáns of the Ottoman Turks have succeeded Ertoghul in the male line without a break.

Ertoghul died in 1288 and 'Uthmán became head of the clan; in the same year Orkhan, son of 'Uthmán, was born. The years of the earlier manhood of 'Uthmán had been peaceable ones, during which he established a reputation for administrative ability and for justness in his rule. At the beginning of the fourteenth century the Seljúk empire which was split up into ten states had begun to fall into decay. Many of its feudatory vassals aspired to independent rule over domains of their own. 'Uthmán remained firm in his allegiance and as a reward, in 1295, the Seljúk Sulṭán 'Alá'u'd-dín Kaikobad II made him a ruler over a territory he had that year conquered, and presented him with the horse-tail, drum and banner, which were the insignia of independent rule. His name was now inserted in the Friday prayers. The date 1295 may be considered to mark the beginning of the Ottoman empire. Gradually, however, the Ottomans began to absorb the domains of the Seljúks, but the process was not completed till some years after 'Uthmán's death. When the Seljúk dynasty had become extinct, there was no power left sufficiently strong to curb the ambition of the Ottomans, though the stronger among the ten states which arose out of the Seljúk empire successfully resisted them for a time.

The Ottomans now turned their attention to the easier work of invading the neighbouring Christian lands, and the conflict with the Greek emperor began in earnest. The inroads were frequent and each campaign attracted volunteers to 'Uthmán's service and increased the number of his captives. As the Mongols had so frequently done, he did not after such forays return to a pastoral life, but fortified the places he had captured and so showed his intention of remaining in the newly conquered territory. After years of warfare, the city of Brusa [1] was captured in 1326. 'Uthmán was now in his

[1] Brusa is situated thirteen miles south of the Sea of Marmorá. It was the capital of the ancient kingdom of Bithynia. The population now is about 37,000.

last illness, but he lived long enough to know that his standard had been planted in the city he had so long wished to capture, and which now became the capital of his growing kingdom. He was buried within its walls. He was the real founder of the Ottoman empire and each successive Sulṭán is girded with the sword of 'Uthmán, preserved in Constantinople for that purpose.

'Uthmán was succeeded by his son Orkhan (1326–59). The Christian inhabitants of Brusa were spared their lives on payment of a ransom of thirty thousand crowns of gold. A mosque and a college were built, and Arabic and Persian scholars of repute were invited to the city which now became the capital of the Ottomans.

'Uthmán had two sons 'Alá'u'd-dín and Orkhan. The latter, though the younger son, became the ruler on account of his martial vigour. Having established himself at Brusa, he paid little attention to the smaller states which had arisen in Asia out of the late Seljúk kingdom, preferring to attract the members of them by the superior organization of his own territories and by victorious campaigns against the Greeks, which in due time he undertook. At first, he directed his time and energies to the capturing of the Greek strongholds in Asia. In a few years Nicomedia, Meacea and Pergamos were added to his dominions, and after the defeat of the emperor Andronicus the Ottoman kingdom extended to the shores of the Hellespont, and the Byzantines retained in 1338 only two towns—Ala Shair and Rega. Orkhan behaved well to the people of the conquered cities. When Meacea was taken, the people were allowed to retire with all their goods; an act of clemency which won the admiration of the Greeks for their conqueror.

Having thus gained control of the whole of the north-west corner of Asia Minor and the command of one shore of the Bosphorus, Orkhan was content to rest for a while. He now saw clearly that the conquest of the Byzantine empire would be arduous and prolonged, and that the best way to ensure final success was to consolidate his dominions, improve his administration, and organize an efficient army. In these endeavours twenty years of peace passed by. 'Alá'u'd-dín was appointed Vizier, and it is to his efforts that the success of the administration and the formation of an army were largely due.

The old plan had been for the chiefs of the clans to summon their men to war, and when the campaign was over the soldiers returned home and pursued their avocations. This plan was now changed entirely. Instead of this somewhat uncertain and untrained force a standing army was formed in which besides the Ottomans, many Seljúks and members of other nomad tribes were enrolled. A paid corps of infantry, called the Piyade was formed. Their wages were small, but they were given lands on the condition that they were always ready for active service. They were rude soldiers and not always amenable to discipline ; so a regiment one thousand strong was formed from the boys of the Christian families conquered in the wars and made captives. Every year for centuries after a thousand Christian youths were thus taken and trained as soldiers. A special officer, the Tournaji Basha, made periodical visits to all the provinces for this purpose ; later on youths from Albania, Bosaia and Bulgaria were preferred. When the captives were not sufficient the Christian subjects had to give up their sons until the required number was made up. After 1648 this levy ceased as the children of the men enrolled were sufficient for the purpose. The lads were brought up as Muslims, were carefully trained under the strictest discipline and well rewarded when their courage and conduct deserved it. 'Cut off from all ties of country, kith and kin, but with high pay and privileges, with opportunities for military advancement and for the gratification of the violent and the sensual passions of their animal natures, this military brotherhood grew up to be the strongest and fiercest instrument of imperial ambition, which remorseless fanaticism, prompted by the most subtle statecraft, ever devised upon earth.'[1]

[1] Creasy, *History of the Ottoman Turks* (ed. London, 1854), vol. i, p. 23.

Thus the famous corps of the Janissaries was formed in the year 1328. The Sulṭán sought religious sanction for his action. The services of a venerable Shaikh of the Baḳtáshiyya Order of Derwishes were called in, and Ḥájjí Baktásh blessed the boys by putting the sleeve of his robe on the head of one of them in such a way that it hung down his back, and then addressing the Sulṭán said: 'The militia which you have just created shall be called Yeni Cheri (new troops); its figures shall be fair and shining, its arm redoubtable, its sword sharp. It shall be victorious in all battles and ever return triumphant.'[1] To commemorate the blessing bestowed by the sleeve of Ḥájjí Baktásh, the Janissaries wore a white felt cap, with a piece of the same material pendant on their backs.

In addition to the Piyade and the Janissaries an irregular force of infantry was formed, whose sad and peculiar duty it was to bear the first brunt of an attack; and when they were cut down or severely treated, the Janissaries rushed on over their dead bodies to attack the now possibly disorganized enemy. A select body of horse soldiers called Sipáhís (Sepoys), who held lands on a feudal tenure, completed the army.

Having now formed this useful army, Orkhan was able to think of further conquests. On the opposite

[1] Sell, *The Religious Orders of Islám*, p. 5.

shore of the Bosphorus was the beautiful city of Constantinople. Naturally his thoughts turned that way. The Byzantine empire had now lost much of its grandeur and much of its power. As a result of civil wars many provinces had been lost, and in Constantinople sedition was rife and rival factions deprived the emperors of any real power. 'The property of the Greeks was plundered, their landed estates were confiscated, and even their families were often sold into slavery. The landed property and the military power, with the social influence they conferred, passed into the hands of the Serbs, the Albanians, the Genoese, and the Ottoman Turks.'[1]

The emperor Cantacuzemus gave his daughter Theodora in marriage to the Sulṭán. In order to secure the aid of the Turks they were permitted to ravage a province,[2] capture as many Christians as they could and sell them as slaves. This they were permitted to do in Constantinople itself, and the

[1] Finlay, *History of Greece*, vol. iii, p. 441, quoted by S. Lane-Poole, *Turkey*, p. 32.

[2] Turks in small bodies had many years previously entered into Europe. In the ninth century some, driven from their homes, obtained from the emperor Theophilus an asylum in Macedonia. They retained their military habits and some formed part of the imperial guard. In the eleventh century another party settled between the Dneeper and the Danube, followed in the twelfth century by another band. They were gradually absorbed into the general population, or kept in check and so gave no serious trouble. See Victor Bérard, *La Turquie* (Paris, 1911), pp. 148–9.

distressed Greeks saw their fellow-Christians of both sexes and of all classes exposed in a public market, and sold to the highest bidder to be henceforth subject to temporal and spiritual bondage. This infamous treaty was the first act in the drama of the downfall of the Byzantine empire. Gibbon thus graphically describes the marriage :—

> A stately pavilion was erected, in which the empress Irene passed the night with her daughters. In the morning Theodora ascended a throne which was surrounded with curtains of silk and gold; the troops were under arms; but the emperor alone was on horseback. At a signal the curtains were suddenly withdrawn, to disclose the bride, or the victim, encircled by kneeling eunuchs and hymeneal torches; the sound of flutes and trumpets proclaimed the joyful event; and her pretended happiness was the theme of the nuptial song, which was chanted by such poets as the age could produce. Without the rites of the Church, Theodora was delivered to her barbarous lord; but it had been stipulated that she should preserve her religion in the harem of Brusa; and her father celebrates her charity and devotion in this ambiguous situation.[1]

Orkhan defeated the enemies of Cantacuzemus, and penetrated the country as far as the Balkans, thus learning how defenceless it was and what an easy prey it would prove to his young and vigorous army. In 1355 Orkhan sent his son Suleymán Pasha with a small force to cross the Hellespont. Other troops followed and the European shore was secured by the Ottomans. The fortress of Gallipole

[1] Gibbon, *Roman Empire* (ed. London, 1855), vol. vii, p. 145.

was taken and other towns were captured. The Ottomans had now come to stay. In 1358 Suleymán was killed by a fall from his horse, the news of which so affected his father Orkhan that he died two months after. He lived long enough to prove the value of his military organization and to test the valour of his new troops. The great merit of all Orkhan's administrative arrangements was that they admitted of development and extension as the empire grew. Long after, when Muḥammad II improved the civil administration he based his reforms on Orkhan's institutions and made them the model of his legislation.

Murád I (1359–89), called Amurath by European writers, succeeded his father. He was a bold and active warrior and soon seized an opportunity of invading Europe. By that time the dominions of the Greek empire had become very much restricted, and many provinces, afterwards included in the Ottoman empire, were under independent princes. This probably postponed the fall of Constantinople for a time, as they had to be first subdued.

Cantacuzemus was now dead and John Palaeologus was emperor. He was utterly incapable of opposing Murád. In 1361 Adrianople was taken and in 1467 it was made the Turkish capital instead of Brusa. Three years later Philippolis fell to the Ottomans. The leaders of the various independent states were now alarmed. These people were far more vigorous than the Greeks; and Murád found in the Serbs, Bosnians, Bulgarians, Albanians and Hungarians valiant and determined foes. In 1364 a contest began, which in modern days has been renewed with entirely different results, for it is the Ottomans who have now lost their pristine vigour. Then an allied army 60,000 strong was beaten by a much smaller Ottoman force under Lála Sháhín, Murád's commander-in-chief.

In 1373 the Turks conquered Macedonia crossed the Balkans and captured Nissa. The king of Serbia had to supply a contingent of troops and to pay a tribute in order to save his kingdom. The ruler of Bulgaria obtained peace by giving his daughter, which apparently he was more ready to do than to part with money. Lála Sháhín was made a feudal lord over these provinces.

About this time Murád returned to his Asiatic dominions to celebrate the marriage of his son Báyazíd, surnamed Yildirim, or Thunderbolt, from the energy he displayed in battle and the quickness of his movements in action. This wedding brought a large accession of territory in the form of a dowry. The absence of Murád in Asia was an opportunity not to be lost, and the Christian princes, vexed at the yearly drain of their boys for the regiment of the Janissaries, and feeling the irksomeness of the tribute required, formed an alliance against the Ottomans, and in Bosnia nearly annihilated one of their armies. Murád and Báyazíd quickly returned and won the great battle of Kosovo in 1382. The Serbs, the Hungarians and others numbered 100,000 men and the conflict was long and fierce. At a council of war it was proposed that the camels of the baggage train should be placed in front to form a living rampart and to confuse the horses of the knights by the smell which proceeded from them. Báyazíd opposed this plan, saying: 'The honour of our flag requires that we should meet the enemy face to face.' His advice was accepted and the camels were sent to the rear. Báyazíd displayed great valour and by his brilliant fighting and rapid movements maintained the reputation of his name Yildirim, or Thunderbolt. The slaughter was great. It was, however, a sad day for the Ottomans, for Milosh Kobilovich, a Serb soldier, gained admittance into the tent of Murád and stabbed him to death with a dagger. Murád lived long enough to give orders for the final charge of his troops and for the execution of Lazarus, the king of Serbia, now a prisoner. The assassin was slain at once, but his work was done and ever since he has been regarded by the Serbs as a hero. His treachery has been overlooked because of the value of its result. It is said that in order to prevent the repetition of such an unfortunate occurrence 'a rule has ever since been prescribed in Ottoman etiquette that no stranger shall be presented to the Sulṭán unless led by two courtiers who hold him by the arms, and thus prevent any treacherous act. This precaution is no longer insisted on; but even in the present (i.e. nineteenth) century ambassadors were not permitted to approach the Sulṭán too closely.'[1]

The result of the defeat at Kosovo was that Serbia became a province tributary to the Sulṭán, although it was allowed to have its own rulers who assumed the title of Despot. This state of things continued for about seventy years, when in 1459 Sulṭán Muḥammad II occupied Serbia and made it a Turkish pashalik. This ignominious position it held for three hundred and forty-five years. In 1804 the struggle for independence began and after long years of conflict it was at length successful.

Constantinople was still spared, but the emperor, John Palaeologus, and his sons had to follow the camp and court of Murád. This humiliation of his rivals satisfied Murád for the present. A show of friendship was maintained and the emperor gave one daughter to Murád and two others to his sons Báyazíd and Ya'qúb Chelebi. Thus these and other princesses played their sorrowful part in the diplomatic game.

Murád's son, Sanji Bey, now governor of Brusa, concerted a plot with Andronicus, son of Palaeologus, to dethrone their respective fathers. It was a

[1] S. Lane-Poole, *Turkey*, p. 45.

foolish thing to do and was soon discovered. Sanji was executed; and the emperor gave orders that his son should be made blind.

Murád was renowned for his courage, for the extension of his empire, and for the love and the fear which his subjects bore towards him.

In the presence of the victorious troops at Kosovo Báyazíd I (1389–1402) was proclaimed Sulṭán. His first act was to give the order for the execution of his brother Ya'qúb Chelebi, who had fought bravely in the recent battle. He remembered how his brother, Sanji Bey, had plotted against Murád and he was determined that there should be no family plot against himself. It set a mournful precedent, for henceforward it became the rule for Sulṭáns on their accession to murder their brothers. There is a text in the Qur'án which says, 'Civil strife is worse than bloodshed' [Súratu'l-Baqara (ii) 214].[1] The action of Báyazíd was probably a straining of this text, but assuming that 'civil strife' was likely to follow, it gave some show of authority for his cruel deed. For many generations this sanction was thus taken and the result of putting out of the way any possible male claimant to the throne has been that revolutions arising from family disputes

[1] الفتنة اكبر من القتل

فتنة (fitna) may also be translated as sedition: Zamakhsharí explains it as 'idolatry'

have not been common. In later times these unfortunate brothers were confined to the harems and grew up ignorant, if not imbecile. The best modern historian of Turkish affairs has said :—

> The progress of civilization has rendered impossible the systematic murder, but not the incarceration of brothers ; and the consequence is that the crown may devolve upon an elderly man, who has been kept a close prisoner all his life and who has no more experience of the world than a monk. If, when the throne is vacant, any prince can, with the aid of the army, seize upon the supreme power, and put his competitors out of the way, his title has generally been accepted ; but there is no trace in Ottoman history of any attempt to dispute the claims of the House of Osman or to establish a rival dynasty. This is clearly a great element of strength compared with the Christian kingdoms with which the Ottoman empire contended during many centuries, and it doubtless did much to counterbalance the many weaknesses which have always been inherent in the Turkish rule.[1]

Báyazíd continued his wars and King Stephen of Serbia was compelled to sue for peace. In the treaty which followed he accepted the position of a vassal, undertook to furnish a contingent of soldiers to render in person military service to the Sulṭán, a task he honourably fulfilled, and to give his sister to the Sulṭán for a wife. This lady was a woman of strong character and influence. It is said of her that 'of all his wives he (Báyazíd) held her dearest, and for her sake restored to her brother the

[1] Odysseus, *Turkey in Europe*, p. 119.

city and castle of Semendria, and Columbarum in Serbia; she allured him to drink wine forbidden by their law and caused him to delight in sumptuous banquets, which his predecessors never did.'[1]

Uskub was taken and Turks settled there as colonists and a feudal system was organized, out of which grew the landed proprietors, afterwards known by the names of Derebeys and Pashas.[2] Wallachia was conquered in the year 1392 and its ruler became a tributary. When all this had been accomplished, the Sulṭán was called to his Asiatic dominions where trouble had arisen. With his usual rapidity he passed from place to place and soon secured possession of all that had belonged to the Seljúk kingdom. To these conquests must be added the possession absolutely, or as tributary states, of many countries in Europe.

He now determined to show to the orthodox Sunní Muslims his respect for the House of 'Abbás and to have a formal religious sanction for the high position to which he had attained. There were now 'Abbásid Khalífas at Cairo,[3] men devoid of real power, kept to give a sort of prestige to the rulers there. From one of these, at the Court of the Mamlúk Sulṭán Burqúq, he was invested with the title

[1] Knolles, quoted by S. Lane-Poole, *Turkey*, p. 49.
[2] See Victor Bérard, *La Turquie*, p. 152.
[3] See Sell, *The Mamlúks in Egypt* (C.L.S.), p. 7.

of Sulṭán.[1] He further showed his religious zeal, by creating a number of religious foundations in the conquered provinces. The Derwish Orders also received much landed property for the support of their zawiyahs (monasteries).[2]

Manuel, the son of the emperor Palaeologus, was serving in the Ottoman army, and on hearing of his father's death, he went away secretly to Constantinople and was proclaimed emperor. This sudden departure was an act of military insubordination which Báyazíd could not overlook, so he returned to Europe, captured Salonica and Larrisa and laid siege to Constantinople; but the formation of a powerful alliance amongst his enemies led to the raising of the siege, and Constantinople was safe for the time.

Sigismund, the king of Hungary, appealed for aid to the Pope, who in 1394 proclaimed a crusade against the Turks. The bravest knights of France and Germany under renowned and princely leaders responded to the call. The Grand Master of the Knights of St. John of Jerusalem came with many followers. An army sixty thousand strong marched through Serbia. King Stephen, faithful to his treaty with the Ottomans (*ante* p. 12), did not join the

[1] As a matter of fact many years before Orkhan had assumed his title; but Báyazíd from political motives sought for and btained this formal religious recognition.

[2] See Victor Bérard, *La Turquie*, p. 158.

Christian army, which in consequence plundered his lands. The Christians then laid siege to Nicopolis, a strong frontier fortress. With an overweening sense of pride, they underestimated the energy of their enemy, and even laughed when news was brought that Báyazíd would soon be upon them. It was so. Then the French knights, against the advice of Sigismund who knew the Ottoman tactics, rushed upon the foe. They easily dispersed the irregular troops whom it was the custom to place in the van. The fury of their onslaught was so great that they succeeded in piercing a second line and thought all was won; but now they found arranged in good order and waiting for them the main body of the Turkish army forty thousand strong. They turned to flee, but it was too late and many lost their lives. The charge was a tactical blunder and its defeat spread dismay amongst the infantry, many of whom fled from the field of battle. The Hungarians and Bavarians made a stand for a time, but Stephen of Serbia brought up his forces and attacked the Christians. Victory fell to the Ottomans.

The battle of Nicopolis (1396) strengthened the power of Báyazíd, but the victory was sullied by the cruelty of the conqueror, who on going over the field of battle said: 'This has been a cruel battle for our people; the Christian have defended themselves desperately; but I will have this slaughter avenged on those who are prisoners.'[1] The next day the whole Turkish army was drawn up in the form of a crescent, and the captives were brought into his presence. He allowed the Count de Nevers to select twenty-four knights to be kept as prisoners until their ransom arrived. Then in their presence and in that of the Sulṭán ten thousand prisoners, knights, squires and soldiers, were brought in and the order for their immediate execution was given. The cruel butchery proceeded until his own officers begged the Sulṭán to let it cease and so a small remnant was left to pass into captivity. The Count de Nevers and his companions were taken about with the army and exposed as trophies, and then confined at Brusa until their ransom arrived.

The pride of Báyazíd now increased and he resumed the siege of Constantinople. It lasted for six years. He had already secured the right to erect a mosque and a college, and to appoint a Qáḍí in the city; now he demanded the entire possession of it. The situation was one of great peril. It was averted not by any courage in its besieged, or loss of vigour in the besiegers, but to a totally unexpected cause—the appearance of Tímúr (Tamerlane) the Tartar in the Asiatic dominions of Báyazíd. He had built up a great empire, was the most renowned monarch of his day, and now it was to come to an end.

[1] Creasy, *History of the Ottoman Turks*, vol. i, p. 62.

Tímúr was born in Samarcund in 1333. From the position of a petty chief he became ruler of the province of Transoxiana. Having under his control vast hordes of men drawn from Central Asia, for thirty years or more he ravaged vast areas of country from Delhi[1] to Damascus. The small kingdoms into which the Muḥammadans were now divided, could not resist, either singly or jointly, the fierce rush of his huge armies. Persia and Syria fell before him; but no less than four attempts against Egypt were successfully met by the bravery of the Mamlúks.

[1] It does not fall within the purpose of this work to describe Tímúr's invasion of India, but a brief note on it will not be out of place. Civil wars and dissensions had weakened the kingdom of Delhi when Tímúr with a large army invaded it. On December 17, 1398, the decisive battle was fought and soon after Delhi was sacked. During the invasion many prisoners were slain, the country was ravaged, the people were massacred, and the victorious troops were laden with spoils. Then Tímúr and his men returned through the hills of Afghánistán and the scourge was over. Years after there was confusion and disorder in the country and the king of Kábul, a descendant of Tímúr, was invited to come and settle the disputes by force of arms. Babar came and conquered (1526); and laid the foundation of the empire which his grandson Akbar made so famous.

More than two centuries passed by and then after the battle of Buxar (Baksar) in 1764 the emperor Sháh Alam signed a treaty by which he and his successors became pensioners of the East India Company. Thus ended the independent political existence of the House of Tímúr.

Again years passed by and after the great mutiny the last Indian sovereign of Tímúr's race, as a deposed monarch, ended his days in exile in Rangoon.

For a time he left Báyazíd alone, but trouble came about in this way. Princes deposed by Tímúr sought refuge with Báyazíd, and some whom Báyazíd had subdued went to Tímúr. Negociations were entered into but Báyazíd's haughty tone gave such offence that Tímúr made war on him. The final issue was decided in the battle of Angora (1402).[1]

Báyazíd appears to have underrated the power of his enemy and learnt his mistake when it was too late. Tímúr was a skilful general who understood the tactical movements of large masses of troops. On this occasion his arrangements were sound, his combinations worked smoothly, his quick eye saw the varrying episodes of a great fight, and his presence was always where it was most needed. Báyazíd was also a capable general, but at a critical moment many of his troops failed him. Amongst them were many inhabitants of the small states which, after the fall of the Seljúks, the Turks had absorbed. These men allured by the promises of the agents of Tímúr broke their allegiance, and saw in the fall of Báyazíd the hope of recovered liberty and the reconstruction of their ancestral countries. Báyazid with his forty thousand Janissaries, supported by the Serbian troops under king Stephen, made a bold

[1] Angora was situated about one hundred and fifty miles east of Brusa.

stand; but, when even his son Suleymán fled and many others had followed, further resistance was hopeless.[1] On the field of Angora the Turks, who then aided the Seljúk chief, first won their renown as warriors (*ante* p. 2) and now, after about a hundred and fifty years had passed, their empire, built up with bravery and ability, was completely ruined, apparently beyond recovery.

Báyazíd was taken prisoner and in a barred litter[2] was carried in the conqueror's train. But, according to Gibbon, Tímúr seems to have dealt kindly with Báyazíd and his son Músá who was also a captive. Báyazíd died in March, 1403, eight months after the battle of Angora, and Tímúr two years after it. During this time, however, Tímúr occupied Brusa and other cities and captured Smyrna from the Knights of St. John, who were then in possession of that city.

[1] For a quaint description of the battle, see Knolles, i. 152, quoted by S. Lane-Poole, *Turkey*, pp. 69-72.

[2] This apparently gave rise to the story related by some Muslim historians to the effect that Báyazíd was carried about in an iron cage. Evliya Efendi says; '"I thank God," said Tímúr, "for having delivered thee into my hand, but if I had fallen into thine what wouldest thou have done." Before his father could reply, Yildirim said: "By heaven! I would have shut thee up in an iron cage, until the day of thy death." Timur replied: "What thou lovest in thy heart, I love in mine."' Then, according to Evliya, Báyazíd was placed in a cage [*Travels of Evliya* (London, 1846), p. 29]. The story is not accepted by later historians as correct.

The Turkish rule in Asia Minor was at an end and the petty princes, dispossessed by them, came into their own again. Seldom has the result of a single battle led to so great a downfall. It would seem as if the history of the Ottoman Turks might have ended here; but it has been well said:—

> The most astonishing characteristic of the rule of the Turks is its vitality. Again and again its doom has been pronounced by wise prophets, and still it survives. Province after province has been cut off the empire, yet still the Sulṭán sits supreme over wide dominions, and is reverenced or feared by subjects of many races. Considering how little of the great qualities of the ruler the Turk has often possessed, how little trouble he has taken to conciliate the subjects whom his sword has subdued, it is amazing how firm has been his authority, how unshaken his power.[1]

It was so now, for within a very few years Muḥammad I, a strong and daring ruler, recovered the lost ground and made the empire stronger than ever. Tímúr checked the Ottomans for a time, but he could not destroy those elements in their character which made for success. Orkhan and his brother (*ante* p. 7) had framed an administrative and military system with much wisdom; the princes of the royal house were well educated, with the result that the men placed in positions of authority were capable and much superior to

[1] S. Lane-Poole, *Turkey*, p. 74.

the officials of the decrepit Greek empire. Stanley Lane-Poole thus describes the situation :—

> It was by their mental as well as physical power that a vast variety of races, both Muḥammadan and Christian, were held together by as firm a grasp as that by which imperial Rome held her provinces; and the standard of the Sulṭán was carried victoriously into the heart of Europe and Asia and far along the shores of Africa. Never was so durable a power reared up so rapidly from such scanty means as were possessed by Orkhan and his Vezir, when they conceived the bold idea of exterminating Christianity by educating Christian children. [1]

Under these circumstances the empire speedily recovered from its fall. After Báyazíd's death, his sons disputed among themselves about the succession. Suleymán, who had fled from the field of Angora, claimed authority in Europe. He was a cruel, dissolute man and was detested by the army; consequently he was soon killed (1410). Músá, another brother, fought the Serbs and then laid siege to Constantinople. The emperor appealed for aid to Muḥammad, another son of Báyazíd. He, assisted by the Serbs, attacked and routed the besieging army and Músá was slain. 'Isá, a third brother, established himself at Brusa, but soon came to an untimely end. When these princes had passed away Muḥammad became sole ruler (1413), and though he only reigned for eight years, in that short time he

[1] *Turkey*, p. 767.

did much to restore the ruined empire to its former greatness.

He was one of the wisest of all the Ottoman Sulṭáns. He found an empire almost ruined by the defeat sustained by Báyazíd, and still further imperilled by the civil discord which arose amongst his sons. Muḥammad, a true statesman, saw that consolidation and not extension was the first result to be secured. In Europe he made friends with the Greek emperor and entered into treaties with other Christian princes. In Asia his difficulties were greater, but he partially overcame them and brought the petty states, which had arisen after the inroad of Tímúr, into subjection. Two acts of cruelty are attributed to him—the blinding of his brother Kásim and the murder of the son of Suleymán, both possible pretenders to the throne. He had experienced the evil of family quarrels and this explains his action, though it does not justify it. Apart from this, he was a mild ruler and sought to bind the various classes of his subjects together in amity and peace. He was a man of cultivated tastes and courteous manners. He earned the name of Muḥammad the gentleman (Chelebi). It was well for the Ottoman empire that such a man had supreme rule in it at such a critical time. He died in 1421 and was buried at Brusa, which, however, was no longer the capital, for Adrianople had taken its place.

Murád II (1421–51) succeeded his father. He found the empire so far recovered from its fall that he was soon able to recommence a career of conquest. It was necessary to assert more strongly than Muḥammad had done the authority of the government in Asia, and so orders were passed for the despatch of an expedition to accomplish this. The death of Muḥammad had been kept secret from the troops, and they refused to go without first seeing him. So the dead monarch's body was propped up in a darkened room, and a servant from behind raised its hands and moved its head as the troops passed by, satisfied with having paid their homage to their master.

Murád declined to pay the subsidy given by Muḥammad to the emperor Manuel, who had released from custody Muṣṭafá a pretender to the Ottoman throne. Muṣṭafá was said to be a son of Báyazíd. This led to a war of rebellion which lasted for a year. Muṣṭafá was taken prisoner and hanged at Adrianople in 1422. Murád was now angry with Manuel for having released Muṣṭafá and laid siege to Constantinople. Báyazíd had done the same, but was obliged to raise the siege and hurry to the defence of his Asiatic dominions. The same thing happened again. Murád had to go rapidly to Asia to quell an insurrection. On his return he left the city alone on the payment of a heavy tribute and the surrender of many towns on the Black Sea coast. In 1428,

Salonica, garrisoned by fifteen hundred Venetians, was captured; its churches were turned into mosques and most of its people were slain or sold as slaves.

But a formidable combination of Christian states was now made, and Murád was soon called upon to show his martial vigour. In 1427 Stephen Lazarevich, the king of Serbia died. He had faithfully kept his compact with the Ottomans and, as we have seen, rendered valuable aid on important occasions. His successor, George Brankovich, was a much better patriot and determined to break away from the Ottoman alliance.[1] He was joined by the rulers of Bosnia, Hungary, Poland, Wallachia and Albania, a formidable confederacy.

The chief hero of the war that ensued was John Hunyady, known as the White Knight of Wallachia. According to Gibbon[2] he was a man of humble origin, his father being a Wallachian, his mother a Greek; but a more romantic story is told by a modern historian. 'When king Sigismund of Hungary was fleeing from one of his unsuccessful engagements with the Ottoman armies, he met and

[1] King Stephen left no heirs and appointed George Brankovich as his successor; but Sulṭán Murád claimed the throne, on the ground that his grandmother, Mileva, a daughter of king Stephen and the wife of Báyazíd I was a Serbian princess. The Serbs, declining to acknowledge the legitimacy of a claim based on such a relationship, rejected the demand of Murád, whereupon he invaded their country, and the result was war.

[2] Gibbon, *Roman Empire*, vol. vii, p. 277.

woed the beautiful Elizabeth Morsiney at the village of Hunyadé, and John Hunyady was believed to be the fruit of this consolatory affection.'[1] Whatever his origin was, Hunyady became the most valiant warrior of his time, so dreaded by the Turks that they used his name to frighten their children. He made successful attacks on the Ottomans and crossed the Balkans, in the depth of winter, a type of military march but rarely attempted.[2] The advance was opposed and a severe struggle thus described took place :—

> The Turks had skilfully barricaded the passes, and poured water down the approaches, which froze into an icy wall during the night. The passage seemed impracticable. Yet nothing daunted, and braving the weapons of the Turks with the same inflexibility as the rigours of the cold, the Hungarians forced the pass of Isladí, and kept Christmas on the southern slope of the famous range.[3]

The Ottomans were defeated a second time and Murád sued for peace. A ten years' truce was agreed upon and the Sulṭán wearied with the cares of office, abdicated in favour of his son Muḥammad II.

The appeals of the Greek emperor for aid found little response, but Burgundy sent a small force which, uniting with the fleets of Venice and Burgundy, became masters of the Hellespont. They

[1] S. Lane-Poole, *Turkey*, p. 87.

[2] It was done by the Russian General, Gurko, in January, 1878, whose army ascended the slopes by cutting steps in the ice, and descended by sliding down.

[3] S. Lane-Poole, *Turkey*, p. 89.

were not aware of the conclusion of the recent treaty of peace, called the treaty of Szegedin (July 12, 1444), by which Serbia regained independence, and Wallachia was annexed to Hungary. The Pope's legate, Cardinal Julian, used this fact to induce Ladislaus, king of Hungary, to break his oath. He said :—

> Is it thus, that you will desert their expectations and your own fortune? It is to them, to your God, and your fellow-Christians, that you have pledged your faith; and that prior obligation annihilates a rash and sacrilegious oath to the enemies of Christ. His vicar on earth is the Roman pontiff, without whose sanction you can neither promise nor perform. In his name I absolve your perjury and sanctify your arms; follow my footsteps in the paths of glory and salvation; and if still ye have scruples, devolve on my head the punishment and the sin.[1]

The scruples of Hunyady were overcome by the offer to make him king of Bulgaria. Though supported by high ecclesiastical authority and approved by popular consent, it was a most disgraceful proceeding and justified reprisals of the severest kind. An army 20,000 strong soon invaded the Ottoman dominions and many places were taken including Varna. Murád in response to earnest appeals from his people returned to public life and with an army of 40,000 veterans took the field. The legate and Hunyady suggested a retreat, but

[1] Gibbon, *Roman Empire*, pp. 272-3.

Ladislaus I, the Hungarian king, determined to try the fortune of war. A desperate conflict ensued, resulting in the defeat of the Christians at Varna on November 10, 1444, and the death of Ladislaus and of the Legate, Cardinal Julian, who had brought about the disgraceful breach of the treaty of Szegedin made only a few months before. Hunyady escaped. Owing to this great victory, the Ottomans had for some centuries little to fear from the attacks of the European nations.

In order to understand the action of many of the Christian princes we must bear in mind the domineering spirit of the Latin Church which aimed at the subjugation of the Eastern one. The Christians of Bosnia and Serbia would have been brought under the rule of the Latins, had Hunyady won a victory at Varna; but to prevent any such possibility, the rulers of these two states agreed to terms of friendship with the Turks. Murád retired into private life after this; but the Janissaries revolted and his presence was again sought for. Once more he assumed the imperial authority and the Janissaries obeyed the well-known voice of their lord. This time he remained in office until his death in 1451, and so passed away one of the noblest of the Turkish Sulṭáns.

He was succeeded by his son Muḥammad II (1451–81) who, on account of his successful siege of Constantinople, has been named the Conqueror.

Unlike Murád, who was of a noble disposition, whose word could be trusted, whose honour was unsullied, Muḥammad was faithless and cruel. Like many of the Mamlúk Sulṭáns of Egypt he combined great ferocity with a love of learning; he founded colleges and was liberal towards what a Muslim would call good works. Poets who sang his praises were given pensions and annual presents were sent to the famous Persian poet Jámí. He was a great warrior though he did little to extend his dominions, beyond the capture of Constantinople, with the exception of Greece which he annexed in 1460,[1] nor did he conquer the great captains, Hunyady and Skanderbeg, of whom more will be said hereafter. He failed to capture Rhodes, which was gallantly defended by the Knights of St. John. His great feat, however, was the capture of Constantinople in 1453. Báyazíd had built one fort on the Asiatic side of the Bosphorus; Muḥammad erected one on the other side, called Rumelia Ḥiṣár, about five miles above Constantinople, and thus prepared for the important siege. Six thousand men were employed in the work and in forty days

[1] Greece was divided into six military divisions, in each of which Turkish settlers were located who held their lands on a military tenure. The number of mounted men they supplied to the army was seven thousand. Heavy imposts were laid upon the inhabitants, including the jizya, or poll-tax. The tribute of Christian children to recruit the ranks of the Janissaries was peculiarly irksome. This continued until 1676 when the tribute ceased.

the fort was rendered impregnable. The situation was now extremely grave. The rulers of the various Christian Powers held aloof, and the rich inhabitants of Constantinople hid their treasures instead of placing them at the emperor's disposal, a foolish deed thus happily described by Dr. Johnson in his tragedy of *Irene* :—

> The groaning Greeks dig up the golden crowns,
> The accumulated wealth of hoarding ages;
> That wealth which, granted to their weeping prince,
> Had ranged enbattled nations at their gates.

No modern historian has surpassed the brilliant description given by Gibbon of the famous siege. The following is his account[1] of the struggle :—

Of the triangle which composes the figure of Constantinople, the two sides along the sea were made inaccessible to an enemy; the Propontis by nature, and the harbour by art. Between the two waters the basis of the triangle, the land side, was protected by a double wall and a deep ditch of the depth of one hundred feet. Along this line of fortifications, for a distance of six miles, the Ottomans directed their principal attack. In the first days of the siege, the Greek soldiers descended into the ditch or sallied into the field; but they soon discovered that, in the proportion of their numbers, one Christian was of more value than twenty Turks; and after these bold preludes, they were prudently content to maintain their rampart with their missile weapons. Nor

[1] *Roman Empire*, vol. vii, ch. lxviii. In making this long quotation I follow a precedent set by S. Lane-Poole the author of *Turkey*, in which Gibbon's description is given at length (ch. vii, pp. 111-135).

should this prudence be accused of pusillanimity. The nation was indeed pusillanimous and base; but the last Constantine deserves the name of a hero; his noble band of volunteers was inspired with Roman virtue; and the foreign auxiliaries supported the honour of the western chivalry.

Then the Turks, pushing their approaches to the edge of the ditch, attempted to fill the enormous chasm, and to build a road to the assault. Innumerable fascines, and hogsheads, and trunks of trees, were heaped on each other; and such was the impetuosity of the throng, that the foremost and the weakest were pushed headlong down the precipice and instantly buried under the accumulated mass. To fill the ditch was the toil of the besiegers; to clear away the rubbish was the safety of the besieged; and, after a long and bloody conflict the web that had been woven in the day was still unravelled in the night.

A wooden turret of the largest size was advanced on rollers; this portable magazine of ammunition and fascines was protected by a threefold covering of bulls' hides; incessant volleys were securely discharged from the loop-holes; in the front, three doors were contrived for the alternate sally and retreat of the soldiers and workmen. They ascended by a staircase to the upper platform, and as high as the level of that platform a scaling-ladder could be raised by pulleys to form a bridge, and grapple with the adverse rampart.

At the dawn of day, the impatient Sulṭán perceived with astonishment and grief that his wooden turret had been reduced to ashes; the ditch was cleared and restored; and the tower of St. Romanus was again strong and entire. He deplored the failure of his design.

At last five vessels, four of which were from Genoa appeared bearing provisions of grain, wine, oil and vegetables. The Turkish fleet at the entrance of the Bosphorus opposed their entrance, and Muḥammad seated on horseback cheered his mariners by his voice. Gibbon thus records the naval battle :—

The five Christian ships continued to advance with joyful shouts, and a full press both of sails and oars, against a hostile fleet of three hundred vessels ; and the rampart, the camp, the coasts of Europe and Asia, were lined with innumerable spectators, who anxiously awaited the event of this momentous succour. In the Christian squadron, five stout and lofty ships were guided by skilful pilots, and manned with the veterans of Italy and Greece, long practised in the arts and perils of the sea. Their weight was directed to sink or scatter the weak obstacles that impeded their passage ; their artillery swept the waters ; their liquid fire was poured on the heads of the adversaries, who, with the design of boarding, presumed to approach them ; and the winds and waves are always on the side of the ablest navigator. They won the naval victory and anchored securely in the inner harbour of the city. At last on May 29 came the final attack.

At day break, without the customary signal of the morning gun, the Turks assaulted the city by sea and land ; and the similitude of a twined or twisted thread has been applied to the closeness and continuity of their line of attack. The foremost ranks consisted of the refuse of the host, a voluntary crowd, who fought without order or command ; of the feebleness of age or childhood, of peasants and vagrants, and of all who had joined the camp in the blind hope of plunder and martyrdom. The common impulse drove them onwards to the wall ; the most audacious to climb were instantly precipitated ; and not a dart, not a bullet, of the Christians was idly wasted on the accumulated throng.

But their strength and ammunition were exhausted in this laborious defence; the ditch was filled with the bodies of the slain; they supported the footsteps of their companions; and of this devoted vanguard, the death was more serviceable than the life.

In that fatal moment, the Janissaries arose, fresh, vigorous, and invincible. The Sulṭán himself on horseback, with an iron mace in his hand was the spectator and judge of their valour; he was surrounded by ten thousand of his domestic troops whom he reserved for the decisive occasion; and the tide of battle was directed and impelled by his voice and eye.

The first who deserved the Sulṭán's reward was Ḥasan, the Janissary of gigantic stature and strength. With his scimitar in one hand, and his buckler in the other, he ascended the outward fortification; of the thirty Janissaries who were emulous of his valour, eighteen perished in the bold adventure. Ḥasan and his twelve companions had reached the summit; the giant was precipitated from the rampart; he rose on one knee, and was again oppressed by a shower of darts and stones. But his success had proved that the achievement was possible; the walls and towers were instantly covered with a swarm of Turks; and the Greeks, now driven from the vantage ground, were overwhelmed by increasing multitudes. Amidst these multitudes, the emperor, who accomplished all the duties of a general and a soldier was long seen, and finally lost.

The prudent despair of Constantine cast away the purple; amidst the tumult he fell by an unknown hand, and his body was buried under a mountain of the slain.[1] After his death, resistance and order were no more; the Greeks fled towards the city; and many were

[1] His head was cut off and publicly exhibited. It was subsequently embalmed and sent round to the chief cities of Asia. See Creasy, *History of the Ottoman Turks*, p. 136.

pressed and stifled in the narrow pass of the gate of St. Romanus.

It was thus, after a siege of forty-three days, that Constantinople, which had defied the power of Chosroes, the Chagan, and the Caliphs, was irretrievably subdued by the arms of Mohamet the Second. Her empire only had been subverted by the Latins; her religion was trampled in the dust by the Muslim conquerors.

From every part of the capital they flowed into the church of St. Sophia. In the space of an hour, the sanctuary, the choir, the nave, the upper and lower galleries were filled with the multitudes of fathers and husbands, of women and children, of priests, monks and religious virgins. The doors were broken with axes; and as the Turks encountered no resistance, their bloodless hands were employed in selecting and securing the multitude of their prisoners. In the space of an hour, the male captives were bound with cords, the females with their veils and girdles. The senators were linked with their slaves; the prelates with the porters of the church; and young men of a plebeian class with noble maids, whose faces had been invisible save to the Sun and their nearest kindred. The loudest in their wailings were the nuns, who were torn from the altar with naked bosoms outstretched hands, and dishevelled hair.

Thus after a siege of fifty-three days fell the glorious capital of the eastern empire. The Khalífas of Damascus [1] and of Baghdad, and three previous Turkish Sulṭáns had failed to capture it. Muḥammad succeeded in doing that which it had long been the aim of many Muslim rulers to accomplish. The emperor, Constantine Palaeologus, the last and

[1] See Sell, *The Umayyad and the 'Abbásid Khalifates* (C.L.S.), p. 33.

noblest of the Caesars, died a brave and honourable death, in striking contrast to the weak and cowardly Musta'ṣim bi'lláh,[1] the last 'Abbásid Khalífa, at the sack of Baghdad in 1258; in its day as memorable an event as the fall of the capital of the ancient Byzantine empire two centuries after.

What was the effect of the capture of Constantinople upon the Sulṭánate? It transformed a chieftain and military leader into an emperor. The Turks looked upon Constantinople as the capital of the world and felt their own importance increased by their occupation of it. The Greek emperors had assumed to themselves, as by divine right, the leadership of Christendom. The Turks sought to emulate their example and, in course of time, the Sulṭáns became *de facto*, though not *de jure*, the Khalífas of the Islàmic world. The simplicity of the camp life was changed for the pomp and luxury of an oriental court. This was one among many causes which finally led to the decline of the Ottoman empire.

Muḥammad increased his European dominions by the conquest of a great part of Serbia, with the exception of Belgrade. Flushed with the conquest of Constantinople, he looked upon the capture of Belgrade as an easy task. He was mistaken. The garrison made a gallant resistance under John Capistran and Hunyady. On July 21, 1456, the

[1] *The Umayyad and the Abbásid Khhalifates*, pp. 106, 108.

great assault was made, the Janissaries carried the trenches and advanced within the walls, only to be repelled by the courage of the besieged. Then Capistran, filled with a fiery zeal, led his men right into the Turkish camp, and they carried all before them. In all this he was ably seconded by Hunyady, before whose troops the Turkish army fled, defeated and depressed. Hunyady survived this crowning triumph of his career less than a month; and shortly after John Capistran also passed away. In after years he was canonized by the Pope for his valiant deeds, which well deserved the veneration of Christendom, and which are remembered in Belgrade, that city of many sieges, to this day.

Bosnia was also attacked and the king and his sons gave themselves up on condition that their lives should be spared. Muḥammad with the consent of his chief legal adviser broke his promise and the king was assassinated. His progress further north was arrested by the bravery of Hunyady. In Albania he was long and successfully opposed by Skanderbeg (Iskender Beg—Prince Alexander) the national hero of the Albanians.

I give a short account of this remarkable man. His father was the hereditary prince of a district in Albania, who had to pay tribute to the Sulṭán and in 1423 to deliver up to Sulṭán Murád II his four sons as pledges of his fidelity. They were made Muslims. The one with whom we are now concerned was well educated, trained for the army and promoted to high rank. He was a great favourite with Sulṭán Murád. When his father died, his brothers were poisoned and the principality was annexed by the Turks. Skanderbeg, however, dissembled his resentment at this cruelty and injustice and patiently abided the time when he could become an independent ruler in his own land. In 1443 he found his opportunity. He deserted his post, and by an act of treachery, involving murder, he gained possession of Croca the chief city in Albania, and proclaimed himself a Christian. Murád sent three expeditions against him and they all failed. Muḥammad succeeded no better and in 1461 concluded a treaty by which Skanderbeg was recognized as the independent ruler of Albania. For five and twenty years he kept his country free and so prevented the Turkish advance into Italy. After his death in 1467 his son and successor sold Albania to the Venetians, who in 1478 resold it to the Turks. It then became a Turkish province, unruly from the first days until now when the doubtful gift of autonomy has been granted to it.

The Venetian republic was next attacked but saved by a treaty made in 1479, which was much to its disadvantage. Greece, some of the islands in the Aegean, and Sinope and Trebizond in the Black Sea became part of the Turkish empire.

The Turks had now begun to form a navy and a powerful expedition was sent to capture Rhodes in 1480, but owing to the bravery of the Knights of St. John it entirely failed. One result, however, of this war was that the Turks gained command of the sea. During the sixteenth and seventeenth centuries no Christian flag was allowed to navigate the Euxine. 'All knowledge of its shores was lost, its cities lay beyond the sphere of trade and the countries once frequented by Genoese and Venetian merchants became as much a region of mystery as they had been before Jason made his voyage in search of the Golden Fleece.'[1] The Turks also had a great fleet in the Mediterranean and were thus enabled to land a force in the year 1480 on Italian soil and stormed Otranto, a fort near Brindisi, many of the inhabitants of which were cruelly put to death. The Sulṭán intended to follow up this initial success, for in the words of Gibbon 'his lofty genius aspired to the conquest of Italy and the same reign might have been decorated with the trophies of the new and the ancient Rome.'[2]

Sulṭán Muḥammad was more than a warrior, he was a distinguished administrator;[3] and a brief account of the political system which, based on that

[1] Finlay, *History of Greece* (London, 1856), p. 125.

[2] Gibbon, *Roman Empire*, vol. vii, p. 340.

[3] 'Muḥammad II was one of those great men whose personal conduct, from their superiority of talent and firmness of purpose, modifies the course of public events, when it is granted to them, as it was to him, to exercise their influence during a long period of time.' Finlay, *History of Greece* (London, 1856), p. 19.

of previous rulers, was perfected by him will be of interest. The Institutes of Muḥammad in their figurative language describe the empire under the metaphor of a tent. The 'lofty door of the royal tent' denotes the chief seat of government. In Italian this is *La Porta Sublima* from which we have the 'Sublime Porte' by which to this day the Turkish Government is known. The state is represented as being supported by four pillars: the viziers, the judges, the treasurers, the secretaries. The viziers were four in number, the chief of whom was the Grand Vizier. The council of state was known as the Divan, with its many officials. The provincial administration was in the hands of Beys and Derebeys who held land on a feudal tenure. At first the term Pasha was a title of honour, but gradually it became limited in its use and practically synonymous with the rank of a military leader, or the office of a civilian governor. The land of a conquered country was divided into three parts. The first was set aside for the support of mosques and other pious foundations. Such property was waqf, that is, reserved for religious purposes, and could not be alienated. A second part became the private property of the individuals into whose possession it came. If the owner was a Muslim he paid tithes; if a Christian a tax on the land, called kharáj and in addition the jizya, or poll-tax. The third portion was subdivided into many parts.

Some went to the Sulṭán and his family; some to various officials and some to the holders of military fiefs. A fief often contained from three to five hundred acres. The owner had to supply when required a number of horsemen for the army. A Sandjak Bey had to bring into the field more than twenty fully-armed horsemen, the *Ziams* any number between four and nineteen, the Timariots came alone or with two or three followers.[1] These fiefs were held as hereditary property.

The feudal system in Europe grew up under comparatively weak rulers; in Turkey it came into existence under strong and vigorous ones. The result was that in the former case it resulted in the growth of a powerful aristocracy; in the latter it did not. The reasons for this striking difference seem to have been: (1) the Sulṭáns during the period of the rise of the empire were vigorous, energetic and able men; (2) the religious system of Islám exalts the position of the ruler but maintains a feeling of equality between his subjects; (3) the absence of any deep-seated desire for popular assemblies.

The feudal system was used for national defence, but, whether for good or ill, seems to have had little influence on the administration of the country.

[1] For an exhaustive description of the military contingents due from each fief, see *The Travels of Evliya* (London, 1846), pp. 101–3.

Later on, when the era of feeble Sulṭáns set in, these feudal lords—the Derebeys—became hereditary chiefs and a powerful aristocracy owning little allegiance to the central government and had finally to be suppressed by Sulṭán Muḥammad in the nineteenth century.

Muḥammad II looked upon the 'Ulamá'[1] as an important body of men learned in dogmatics and law, from whom religious teachers and legists were drawn. They were organized into a distinct body, and arrangements were made for their education and training. They were treated with honour by the government and so, as professors and judges, commanded the respect of the people. Schools, from the simple maktabs, or elementary schools, and colleges were founded. The whole system of education was good and suitable for its purpose. The regulations for the non-Christian subjects were those common to all Muslim countries. They were Dhimmís, that is, they were allowed to live on payment of a poll-tax. Under fanatical rulers their lot was a hard one, but generally speaking they were fairly well-treated, except in the matter of the tribute of their children for the corps of Janissaries.

When the Ottoman empire was powerful conversions to Islám were frequent, and such renegades were often promoted to high offices. During the

[1] Plural form of 'Álim, a learned man.

reigns of Suleymán I and Salím II out of ten Grand Viziers eight were renegades.[1]

In addition to all these important matters of administration Muḥammad gave personal attention to the rules for ceremonial etiquette, police regulations, and the criminal law. The regulations for these were codified under his supervision. This code is known as the *Muleka'u'l-Abḥár*—The Confluence of Seas—a name which expresses the comprehensiveness of its enactments. It was for a long time, and may be still, an important legal code in the Ottoman empire.

I conclude this notice of the administration of Muḥammad II by a quotation from his Institutes which shows that amidst much that was admirable there was that which is inhuman and detestable. It is thus recorded :—

> The majority of my jurists have pronounced that those of my illustrious descendants who ascend the throne may put their brothers to death, in order to secure the repose of the world. It will be their duty to act accordingly.[2]

Prince Jem (Jemshid), the older and abler of Muḥammad's two sons, a man who possessed his father's vigour and was courteous and cultured, did

[1] For an account of the skilful way in which Muḥammad dealt with the Greek clergy, see Finlay, *History of Greece* (London, 1856), pp. 161-4.

[2] Von Hammer, *Geschichte Osmanischen Reiches* (Buda-Pesth 1835), book xvii.

not hear of his father's death until Báyazíd had reached Constantinople and secured the allegiance of the Janissaries, and so Báyazíd II ascended the throne. He had to reward the Janissaries, and this led to the establishment of the custom of the accession-bakshish, granted to them when a new Sulṭán came to the throne. His long reign (1481–1512) was not a glorious one, for the Sulṭán was a very lethargic and incompetent ruler. Prince Jem contested the succession for a year, but was beaten and found refuge with the knights of Rhodes, to whom Báyazíd, after some vain attempts to come to terms with Jem, paid a large sum of money to keep Jem a prisoner. The knights then sent him to one of their settlements at Nice. The various European rulers were anxious to gain possession of the prince. Charles VIII of France took Jem away from the knights and consigned him to the custody of Pope Innocent VIII, who then agreed to keep him safe, and received for so doing the sum of 40,000 ducats a year from Báyazíd. During the long years of Jem's captivity many kings and princes held out hopes of his restoration to the Sulṭánate and indeed it was this which Báyazíd feared. The next Pope, Alexander Borgia, demanded a lump sum down for his work as jailer. Then the king of France again intervened and took possession of the unhappy Jem; but it is said that Borgia in revenge caused Jem to be poisoned. Some, however, say he died of grief in 1494. Whichever story is true the whole transaction was shameful. For the sake of money the head of the Church and the Grand Master of a great Order betrayed a man worthy of all the support they could give him. It was a disgraceful act in the intercourse of Christendom with Turkey. In captivity Prince Jem occupied his time in composing poetry, of which the following is a specimen :—

> Bird of my soul, be patient of thy cage,
> This body, lo! how fast it wastes with age,
> The tinkling bells already do I hear
> Proclaim the caravan's departure near ;
> Soon shall it reach the land of nothingness
> And thee, from fleshly bonds delivered, bless.

In the north there were frequent wars with varying success to either side. A war with Sháh Ismá'íl of Persia gave some trouble. The Mamlúks of Egypt also waged war upon the Turks in Asia. Báyazíd's later years were troubled by the dissensions among his sons. Salím the younger and most vigorous of them, supported by the Janissaries, attacked his father's troops at Adrianople, and caused him to abdicate in his favour. Báyazíd died soon after to the great relief of the rulers and people of the neighbouring states.

Salím I (1512–20) had two brothers alive, and several nephews. He determined to put them all away. He watched from a window the murder of five nephews. Being thus secure from domestic strife he turned his attention to his eastern dominions. He first attacked the Safavid monarch Sháh Ismá'íl, the head of the Shí'ah Muslims. The contest was long but in the battle of Cháldirán (1514) the Turks won a great victory, captured Tabríz, and sent a thousand of its skilled workmen to Constantinople. Salím had made a vow that, if he won a victory over Shí'ah Persians, he would build three grand mosques—one at Jerusalem, another in Buda and a third at Rome; but his death prevented the fulfilment—or attempt at fulfilment—of his vow. After the Persian campaign he resolved to wrest Egypt from the Mamlúks. In this he was successful, and thus nearly doubled the extent of the Ottoman dominions. Egypt became a province of Turkey, and the rule of the Mamlúk Sulṭáns came to an end. The Mamlúks as a separate body, however, remained under their Shaikhu'l-Beled, or Mayor, a powerful community and often gave trouble to the Turkish governor.

The Mamlúks had revived the 'Abbásid Khalífate in Cairo,[1] and Salím brought away with him to Constantinople, the Khalífa, Mutawakkil, who made over to him his spiritual authority, such as it was, and Salím became the Khalífa of Islám. Mutawakkil had no authority whatever to do this, for none but a member of the Arab tribe of the Quraish

[1] See *The Mamlúks in Egypt* (C.L.S.) pp. 6-9.

should hold this office. He also gave up the symbols of the office, the sacred banner and cloak of the Prophet, which are still preserved in the Seraglio at Constantinople. However, whatever he was *de jure*, Salím became *de facto* the Khalífa over all the orthodox section of Muslims who elect to own his authority. The office is now shorn of any real power, but it adds somewhat to the prestige of the Sulṭáns of Turkey, some of whom, such as ‘Abdu’l-Ḥamíd I, have in vain tried to use it to foster a pan-Islámic movement.

When Muḥammad II captured the island of Lesbos in 1462 he left there a soldier named Ya‘qúb, whose two sons, Urúj Barbarossa and Khairu’d-dín,[1] became successful mariners and famous Corsairs. Soon after the conquest of Egypt, Salím received messengers from Khairu’d-dín, asking for his favour and protection, offering in return to make over the province of Algiers which he had won. The Sulṭán was delighted, accepted the proposal, and so added a new and valuable province to his African dominions (1519). The bold Corsair was made Beglerbeg (governor) of Algiers and invested with

[1] ‘It is possible that Barbarossa is but a European corruption of Baba Urúj or Father Urúj, as his men called him. At all events Urúj is the real Barbarossa, though modern writers generally give the name to his younger brother, Khairu’d-dín, who was only called Barbarossa on account of his kinship to the original.’ S. Lane-Poole, *The Barbarry Corsairs*, p. 38, foot-note.

the insignia of office—the horse, the sword, and the horse-tail banners.

Salím, a bold and vigorous warrior, was cruel in his disposition and practice. In the year 1514 he ordered the massacre of forty thousand Shí'ahs and then prepared to murder the Christians. He asked the Shaikhu'l-Islám whether the conversion of the nations to Islám was better than their conquest. The answer was in the affirmative. To the horror of his advisers the Sulṭán then ordered that all Christians should be slain and that their churches should be turned into mosques. The Shaikhu'l-Islám, who had not expected that his reply would be thus interpreted, with great difficulty saved the lives of the Christians; but could not preserve their churches, though he gained permission for them, on the loss of their beautiful sanctuaries, to worship in mean and inferior buildings.

The next Sulṭán was Suleymán the Magnificent (1520-66). He rightly deserves this name for his long reign was one of the most brilliant in Turkish history. It was a century of great rulers—Charles V, Francis I, Elizabeth, and Akbar—and amongst them all Suleymán held no second place. It has been well said:—

> The most remarkable feat that the Turks achieved during the glorious century was that they survived it. With such forces as were arrayed against them, with Europe roused from its long sleep, and ready to seize arms and avenge its long disgrace upon the infidels, it

was to be expected that the fall of the Ottoman power must ensure. Instead, we shall see that this power was not only able to meet the whole array of rejuvenated Europe on equal terms, but emerged from the conflict stronger and more triumphant than ever.[1]

Muḥammad II had failed to capture Belgrade or to get possession of the island of Rhodes. Suleymán succeeded in securing both. Belgrade was then fortified more strongly and the possession of it brought Venice as a humble suppliant, willing as the price of safety to become the Sulṭán's vassal. Now that Egypt was a part of the empire, it became highly necessary to secure Rhodes in order to get command of the sea, and so in 1522 a powerful expedition of over a hundred thousand troops was despatched. The Turkish troops were skilled in attacking fortified positions and possessed artillery far superior to that of their opponents; so the siege was prosecuted with great vigour. The garrison consisted of 5,000 men, of whom 500 were knights. The seamen of the port and the citizens rendered valuable assistance, but the Grand Master and his knights looked in vain for succour from Europe, and so after a brave defence of several months they capitulated on honourable terms, being allowed to depart with weapons and property. They retired to Malta, which shortly after they successfully defended against Suleymán. The Sulṭán had a personal

[1] S. Lane-Poole, *Turkey*, p. 166.

interview with the Grand Master, Villiers de L'Isle Adam, a French knight of renown, and expressed to him his regret at having to make him leave his ancient home at Rhodes. The valour of the knights had won the admiration of the Ottomans and the armorial bearings on their houses were not defaced and some of them may be seen even to this day. The inhabitants of Rhodes also received good terms, for Suleymán could be a generous victor. They were to have unrestricted liberty as regards religion, and were exempted from the payment of tribute for five years.

A short period of peace followed in which the Sulṭán attended to the internal affairs of the empire. An attempt to curtail the large donations to the Janissaries led to trouble with that masterful and turbulent body. The best way to keep them quiet was to find them warlike occupation and the chance of securing booty. This plan was supported by the able Vizier Ibráhím. This wise and prudent official, in whom the Sulṭán placed implicit trust, had been captured as a lad by Corsairs, sold as a slave and passed into the service of Prince Suleymán when he was a provincial governor. Ibráhím became an accomplished scholar and an amusing entertainer, and so rapidly rose in his master's favour until he reached the high office of Vizier. When Suleymán became Sulṭán, Ibráhím strongly urged the war against Hungary which took place in 1526.

The Turkish army, 100,000 strong with three hundred guns, marched out from Belgrade, crossed the Danube, took several cities and finally on the field of Mohacs (August 28, 1526), defeated the Hungarian army under king Louis II. The Hungarian force was much smaller than that of the Turks, but they rushed boldly to the attack and easily overcame the first line of the opposing army. They had forgotten the Ottoman tactics of placing inferior troops in the van (*ante* p. 8) and thought that victory was near, but behind the retreating troops were three hundred guns and the famous corps of the Janissaries. The result was a most disastrous defeat for the Hungarians. Twenty thousand men perished. The king, bishops and archbishops, and a great number of lords and many nobles gave up their lives on the fatal field of Mohacs. Buda and Pesth were occupied; the country round was ravaged; and one hundred thousand captives were taken away to be sold as slaves. The great library in the palace of Hunyady's famous son Matthias,[1] one of the ablest kings of Hungary, was taken to Constantinople.[2] The defeat at Mohacs ruined Hungary and petty strife amongst the nobles ensued, the result of which was that for a hundred

[1] For an account of this great ruler, see Vambery, *Hungary*, ch. x.

[2] Vambery says the library was burnt (*Hungary*, p. 289); but on p. 295 he says part of it was taken to Constantinople.

and forty years. Hungary became a province of the Turkish empire.

Then began a dispute with the emperor Charles V.[1] The Turks appointed Zapolya who had been the Voyvode of Transylvania as the nominal king of Hungary; but the Archduke Ferdinand, brother of the emperor Charles, claimed the throne. Francis I of France, not wishing to see the emperor's power increased, urged the Turks to withstand Ferdinand's claim. Zapolya appealed to Suleymán, who resolved to interfere in this civil war. He declined all overtures made by Ferdinand and again took the field with an enormous army; he recaptured Buda which for a hundred and forty years onwards was controlled by the Turks. He also restored Zapolya to his throne.

The Sulṭán now determined on a bold stroke and advanced to besiege Vienna. His irregular cavalry devastated the country through which they passed, plundering and destroying all they could lay hands on, and carrying off men, women and children into captivity. Meanwhile, Austria made great efforts to meet the danger, and Vienna was provisioned and made ready for a siege. Houses were destroyed

[1] King Louis died without leaving a son and heir. By an ancient law of Hungary only a native prince could reign, and on this law Zapolya based his claim. Ferdinand was brother-in-law to Louis and on that relationship and also on a treaty claimed the throne.

near the wall, which was strengthened in its weakest parts and entrenchments were made on the banks of the Danube. Non-combatants were sent away and many fell victims to Suleymán's ruthless soldiers whom they encountered in their fight.

The garrison of Vienna consisted of less than twenty-five thousand men; but they were brave and determined. They successfully repelled all assaults and maintained excellent spirits.[1] Suleymán had once made a vow that he would breakfast in Vienna, and now as the attack went on and was successfully met, the Viennese sent to tell him that his breakfast was getting cold. The last assault led by the Janissaries failed and the siege which had lasted three weeks was raised (October 14, 1529). It was 'a famous day in German history: it is the anniversary of the peace of Westphalia and of Vienna, the battles of Hochkirchen, Jenu and Leipsic and of the capture of Ulm.'[2] Four years after, peace was made (1533) and Hungary was divided between Zapolya and Ferdinand. The peace did not last long and another war was made, which ended in Ferdinand's consenting to pay a large annual tribute. A five years truce was then made, after which hostilities recommenced and continued during the rest of the Sulṭán's life.

[1] For a good account of the defence of Vienna, see Creasy, *History of the Ottoman Turks*, pp. 269–74.

[2] S. Lane-Poole, *Turkey*, p. 191.

Meanwhile the Shí'ah subjects of the empire in Asia had been giving very much trouble; but Suleymán very soon put the revolt down, captured Baghdad in 1534, and then annexed the whole country of Armenia. Successful by land, the Sulṭán also asserted his power at sea under his famous admiral Khairu'ddín. This brought him into conflict with Venice.

In Suleymán's reign the naval power of the Ottomans increased rapidly. Urúj Barbarossa was dead, but his brother Khairu'd-dín, also called Barbarossa, was a man of great courage and determination. He had been appointed Governor-General of Algiers by Salím I in 1519, and soon the ports of Barbary passed into his possession and his Corsairs were masters of the sea. Their prizes were rich and numerous, and he rescued many thousands of Moors then in servitude in Spain. Suleymán appreciated the valuable aid which the number and boldness of the Corsairs gave him. He was anxious to see and consult Barbarossa and in 1533 the great Corsair sailed from Algiers to Constantinople, where he was received with much honour. He spent the winter there, improved the build of vessels of war, and in the spring had a formidable fleet of ships ready for sea. He led them into the Straits of Messina, bombarded Reggio, captured many vessels and did damage to the coast towns. He captured Tunis, but was driven away by an expedition sent by Charles V. He then proceeded to Minorca, gained much treasure and many prisoners, all of whom he took to Algiers, and in due course returned to Constantinople. He was now made Captain Pasha, or admiral of the fleet. Meanwhile, the great Genoese admiral, Andrea Doria, was scouring the seas in search of Barbarossa. At last they met, for a war with Venice had broken out. The Venetian fleet was in the Adriatic and Barbarossa in 1538 went to meet it, with one hundred and fifty ships. Many of the most famous Corsairs of the day were with him. The Venetian fleet was much larger, but he was able to anchor in a spacious gulf. He wisely, in view of his inferiority in the number of vessels, determined to wait there till attacked. The Venetian fleet appeared and both watched each other for some time—Doria unwilling to attack; Barbarossa too good a strategist to come into the open. Then Doria sailed away. The Turks could not be restrained and set sail after him. A battle ensued without any decisive result as regards the destruction of either fleet, for Doria again sailed away. Still it was a great moral victory for the Turks. The most renowned admiral of the day, with two hundred ships of war belonging to three great Christian states had sailed away before a smaller Ottoman fleet. Suleymán was delighted when he heard the news, and henceforth for many a long year to come the fleet of the Turkish Sulṭán ruled supreme in the Mediterranean. About the same time another fleet sailed into the Indian Ocean and on the return voyage captured Aden.

Insurrections in Hungary recurred for some years and in 1547 Sulṭán Suleymán, the emperor Charles and king Ferdinand signed at Adrianople a truce for five years, Ferdinand consenting to pay a tribute of 20,000 ducats and to recognize all the Turkish conquests in Hungary. This gave Suleymán some leisure, and he was able to resume his contest with Persia. He gained Armenia and Georgia and captured Erzerum. The conflict lingered on for some years, until in 1555 a treaty was made, the first one ever signed by both Sháh and Sulṭán.

In 1565 Suleymán made an unsuccessful attack on Malta, now held by the Knights of St. John, lately expelled from Rhodes. They fortified the excellent harbours and strengthened the defences. A fleet of one hundred and eighty-one vessels and an army of 30,000 men comprised the expedition. For four months the attack was maintained with vigour and was met by a stubborn resistance. At last in the beginning of September a fleet, sent by the Viceroy of Sicily, appeared and the Turks departed. The failure of this attempt was a cause of much grief to Suleymán.[1]

[1] For a full account of the siege, see Creasy, *History of the Ottoman Turks*, vol. i, pp. 304-9.

Meanwhile irregular fighting went on in Hungary for some years. Then in 1566 Suleymán determined to make a supreme effort to restore order and compel obedience to his will. For the sixth time he invaded Hungary, this time with a force of 200,000 men and three hundred guns. He first attacked the fortress of Szigetvár. Nicholas Zrinyi, the commandant, was a brave man and, after collecting in the fort about two thousand five hundred men and a good stock of provisions, he awaited the attack. The siege was prolonged and Zrinyi would listen to no promises of reward for himself, and was deterred by no severe threats of punishment for his obstinacy. The Sulṭán, wearied with the delay and, perhaps, annoyed at being held at bay by such a puny force, gave orders for a grand assault. It is thus described :—

> The aged ruler, who now but rarely showed himself to his soldiers, mounted his favourite charger and appeared amongst the Janissaries in order to rouse and encourage them. His troops rushed enthusiastically into the fight, for which the artillery and the engineers conducting the siege had made every preparation many days before. But Zrinyi was ready and wide-awake, and drove the assailants back with great slaughter. [1]

Another attack, made a few weeks later on, succeeded, yet even then Zrinyi and his men did not capitulate. He gathered the little band together in the inner fort to which they had

[1] Vambery, *Hungary*, p 315.

retired, praised them for their courage and, saying that the road to death was the road to honour, urged them to show that the conclusion of their heroic career was worthy of their past. The bridge was lowered and Zrinyi and his faithful six hundred followers sallied forth, and after a fierce struggle all but a few soldiers perished. The Turks rushed into the fort, but a mine was exploded which led to a loss of some thousands of men. The rest returned home, after losing 30,000 men in the capture of the city. Zrinyi's fame spread far and wide and won for him the admiration of all Europe.

A few days before the siege was over Suleymán died in camp (September 6, 1566) after a reign of forty-six years. A beautiful elegy by a Turkish poet speaks of his burial thus :—

> He, to the lustre of whose sword the Hunnish paynim bowed ;
> He, whose dread sabre's flash hath wrought the wildered Frank's despair
> Like tender rose-leaf, gently laid he in the dust his face ;
> And earth, the guardian, placed him like a jewel in his case.

He was the greatest of all the Turkish rulers. Wise in administration, just in his dealings, courteous and cultivated, he rightly earned the name of Suleymán the Magnificent. Yet like so many eastern rulers, with all that was commendable and praiseworthy, there was a vein of inhumanity and cruelty in his character. He was personally devoted to his able vizier Ibráhím, and yet one day in 1536 from some cause or other he became jealous of him and put him to death. He married a Russian lady, named Khurrem (Joyous) but known by Europeans as Roxelana. This lady had a son Salím whose chance of becoming Sulṭán was barred by his half-brother Muṣṭafá. At Khurrem's instigation Suleymán had Muṣṭafá slain. Another son Báyazíd and his young children met with a similar fate. These were blots on a great career, marked on the whole by more than the usual wisdom and justice shown by oriental despots.

In his reign the first ambassador from France came to his court (1534), and a year after the first capitulations with France were made.[1] Suleymán

[1] These were afterwards made with other European states. By virtue of the capitulations foreigners do not come sunder the jurisdiction of Turkish courts of law. Their cases can only be tried in consular courts. Cases between foreigners and Turks are tried in Turkish courts, but a consular dragoman is then present to watch the procedure. In modern times, the Turks have tried to do away with the capitulations but the European states would not give way. In 1914, just before the declaration of war between England and Turkey, the Turkish Government, without giving any notice, suddenly abolished them, and that is how the matter stands at present. After the war is over the whole question will be reopened and the action of the Turkish Government will be condoned or repudiated. In the present chaotic state of the Turkish administration it is not probable that the European states will relinquish so necessary a safeguard for the legal protection of their subjects.

left the empire, wealthy, prosperous and extended. The annual revenue was 12,000,000 ducats, which was double that of the great empire over which Charles V ruled. Exports were large, trade was good and the population was increasing. Later on the extortion of the Pashas ruined commerce and decreased the population, and the prosperous days of Suleymán were known no more. In the eastern parts of it were the famous cities of Baghdad, Damascus, Jerusalem, Cairo with many others; in Europe, Constantinople, Adrianople, Athens, Belgrade and Buda. Supreme at sea, the Turkish fleets were masters of the Mediterranean, the Red and the Black Seas. The kings of Europe could not withstand its power by land or sea. Nearly three hundred years had passed away since Ertoghul and his little band of Ottomans first came into notice and now a great and mighty empire had grown from so small a beginning. The Ottoman empire had now reached the height of its fame, and the zenith of its glory. Henceforth, there is decline and decay; but until now it had produced a most remarkable series of rulers, to whose energy and powers of administration, and to whose strong wills, which made subjects obey and enemies fear, the great prosperity of the Ottoman empire is mainly due.

No other dynasty can boast such a succession of brilliant sovereigns as those who conducted the Ottomans to the height of renown in the fourteenth, fifteenth and sixteenth centuries. Orkhan, the taker of Nicaea and founder of the Janissaries; Murád I, the conqueror at Kosovo; Báyazíd I, the victor of Nicopolis; Muḥammad I, the restorer of the shattered empire; Murád II, the antagonist of Hunyady and of Skanderbeg; Muḥammad II, the conqueror of Constantinople; Salím I, who annexed Kurdistan, Syria, and Egypt; and Suleymán the Magnificent, the victor on the field of Mohacs and the besieger of Vienna. Never did eight such sovereigns succeed one another (save for the feeble Báyazíd II) in unbroken succession in any other country; never was an empire founded and extended during two such splendid centuries by such a series of great rulers. In the hour of dismay, as well as in the moment of triumph, the Turkish Sulṭán was master of the situation.[1]

Still what has been so well said of Turkish rule in India, is also true of the rule of the Ottoman Turks in Europe, even in its most brilliant period. It 'does not mean the growth of constitutions, the development of civic rights, the vindication of individual liberty, or the evolution of self-government.'[2]

[1] S. Lane-Poole, *Turkey*, p. 78.

[2] S. Lane-Poole, *Mediæval India*, p. 60.

II. THE DECLINE OF THE EMPIRE

SULEYMAN was succeeded by his son Salím II (1566-74). We now enter upon a period of decline, arrested now and then by a brief period of recovery. The Sulṭáns of the past had been brave warriors and skilful administrators, who kept their vast dominions in order and extended them. Their successors with a few exceptions were weak, degenerate men, who preferred the joys of the harem to the stern realities of the battle field.[1] They lost the esteem of the army which did what the body-guards in Baghdad had done—set up and deposed Sulṭáns at its will. With effeminate Sulṭáns, incompetent officers and corrupt administrators, it is no wonder that the decline was real and persistent. It is only another example of what always takes place in Muslim states. It was so in the latter days of the 'Abbásid Khalífate in Baghdad, in

[1] They are thus described by a Muslim writer: 'Instead of identifying themselves with the life of their people and priding themselves on being the light that guided them, the Sulṭáns now retired into the harems and gave themselves up to a life of ease and indulgence utterly foreign to the habits and principles of their great predecessors.' 'Alí Haidar Midhat Bey, *The Life of Midhat Pasha* (London, 1903), p. 14.

Spain at the close of the Umayyad Khalífate, in Cairo when the early and strong Mamlúk rulers like Beybars gave place to weak and inefficient men, and in India in the last days of the decrepit Delhi rulers.

Salím II was surnamed the Sot; but so well had the empire been organized by his great father that it could not suddenly fall to pieces. He had the good fortune to possess in Muḥammad Sokolli an efficient Vizier. Arabia was subdued, Cyprus was captured and Tunisea became a Turkish province. The Pope, Venice and Spain now united, and an allied fleet under Don John of Austria, who had already won fame in the wars against the Moors in Spain, met and defeated the Turkish fleet at Lepanto in 1571. The latter was the stronger force, but after a severe conflict ninety-four Turkish vessels were sunk and over a hundred were captured. This great victory did away with the idea that the Turkish fleet was invincible; but its material effect was small. Venice withdrew from the alliance and made a separate peace, and a new Turkish fleet was soon got ready for sea. It was under the command of Ochiali, the last of the great Corsairs. He recaptured Tunis which Don John had taken in 1573, but nothing permanent followed from this transient revival of naval power.

Murád III the next Sulṭán (1574–95) was a very inefficient ruler. His first public act was to order the assassination of his five brothers. Though he kept Sokolli in office he was jealous of him and often thwarted his plans. Other able men were set aside for those who purchased their appointments, or were promoted through harem influence. The corps of Janissaries now grew in strength to 48,000 men, as the regulations regarding admission were much relaxed. Under the rule of a weak Sulṭán, the growing power of this turbulent body of men was a standing menace.

Next to the dowager Sulṭána, or as that lady is usually called in Turkish the Sulṭána Valida, the lady who had most influence over Murád was a foreigner. Murád took as one of his wives a Venetian captive lady, Ṣafiyya, who exercised over her husband and then over his son and successor great influence, which she used always for the promotion of her favourites. She contrived, however, to keep the Sulṭán on good terms with Venice. It was during this reign that the first British embassy was sent to Constantinople (1589) with the view of obtaining an alliance with the Turks against Philip II of Spain.

The next Sulṭán was Muḥammad III (1595-1603). As soon as Murád was dead, Ṣafiyya, now Sulṭána Valida, recalled her son Muḥammad from his provincial governorship and had him proclaimed Sulṭán. He was a weak-minded man, though sometimes energetic and more often violent. His father had a family of one hundred and three children, of whom twenty sons and twenty-seven daughters survived him. One of the first acts of Muḥammad was to slay his nineteen brothers and seven enceinte female slaves then in the harem. The political and military affairs of the empire were in almost hopeless confusion and the Sulṭán remained inactive. At last, though against the wishes of his mother Ṣafiyya, he was induced to lead the army in person, as his predecessors had so often done. The Shaikhu'l-Islám warned him of the danger of non-compliance with this request. For a time the tide of war went against the Turks and the Sulṭán betrayed considerable weakness, but in the last conflict victory was secured by the skilful tactics of a renegade named Scipio Cicala. The rest of the reign was quite inglorious, and the Sulṭán's last days were sullied by the murder of his son Maḥmúd, a prince of great promise, who had excited his father's jealousy. The mother of Maḥmúd and all his companions shared his sad fate. The Sulṭán died on December 22, 1603, unregretted and unlamented.

The courageous conduct of Scipio Cicala at the battle of Cerestes saved the empire from disaster. This young man was the son of an Italian Count who owned a fleet of privateers. In one of his forays he captured a number of Turkish ladies and married one of the most beautiful of them, who was baptized under the name of Lucretia. Her son

Cicala, in after years, was taken prisoner by the Turks. He embraced Islám, rapidly rose to high office and married the daughter of Sulṭán Suleymán. When he commanded the fleet he visited Sicily and had an interview with his mother. The beautiful woman, once a captive taken from her Turkish home and forcibly converted into a Christian matron, stood by her handsome son, who began his career as a Christian warrior, but was now a mighty champion of the Crescent and the determined foe of the Cross. It would be interesting to know what they felt and said. They never met again. Cicala was one of many renegades who have attained to high office, and in critical times have rendered valuable service to the Ottoman state.

Sulṭán Aḥmad I (1603–17) was a lad of fourteen years of age, when he succeeded his father. His reign is chiefly remarkable for the decline of the haughty tone of superiority the Sulṭáns had used with other potentates. Austria ceased to pay a tribute and its emperor was respectfully named in Turkish documents by his proper official title, while in a treaty he was regarded as an equal monarch.

The next Sulṭán, Muṣṭafá I, reigned only a few months when he was deposed in favour of his brother U͟thmán II (1618–22). The Janissaries, who now elected their own Pasha and so were free from direct imperial control, deposed U͟thmán and put him to death. Muṣṭafá resumed authority but soon resigned in favour of his nephew.

Murád IV (1623–40) was only twelve years old when he ascended the throne, but he soon showed signs of a strong character, fitted to deal with the disorganized state of the empire. In this he was aided by his mother, a woman of great ability and energy. In Asia and in Africa there were wars and revolts. In Constantinople 'there was an empty treasury, a dismantled arsenal, a debased coinage, exhausted magazines, a starving population and a licentious soldiery.'[1] Seldom has a young ruler been called upon to face such adverse conditions. As he grew up to man's estate, he met his difficulties with resolution, and when he attained to power ruthlessly punished his rebellious subjects.

> Every morning the Bosphorus threw up on its shores the corpses of those who had been executed during the preceding night; and in them the anxious spectators recognized Janissaries and Sipahis, whom they had lately seen parading the streets in all the haughtiness of military license.[2]

The Sultán now twenty years old took an active part and showed the utmost bravery in asserting his authority. Unfortunately the severe measures he had to adopt had a bad influence on his nature, and he became a blood-thirsty tyrant. On the least

[1] Creasy, *History of the Ottoman Turks*, vol. i, p. 395.

[2] Ibid., p. 402.

suspicion officials were put to death, and so great was their fear that a summons to the Sulṭán's presence was viewed with the greatest alarm, and before they entered into his chamber, men made the ablutions which usually preceded death. At first he only executed traitors, then suspected officials, and finally any person who excited his displeasure. In his later years he became intemperate and still more ferocious. A favourite saying of his was: 'Vengeance never grows decrepit, though she may grow grey.' He tolerated no crime but his own, and so for the time saved his country. He won a victory over the Persians and captured Baghdad on November 15, 1638, which has remained Turkish to this day. The defence was strong and this so exasperated the Sulṭán that when the city was won, he only spared three hundred men out of a garrison of thirty thousand. The rest perished. He restored the navy, put down an insurrection in Albania and brought an amount of order into the administration which had long been absent from it.

Apart from his capricious cruelty Murád IV was a great Sulṭán and rendered good service to his empire but his cruelties were long remembered. One of his last acts was for no apparent reason to order the death of his brother Ibráhím. The Sulṭána Valida concealed the victim and made the Sulṭán believe that his order has been carried out. It is recorded that Murád then 'grinned a ghastly smile' and tried to rise from his bed to see the corpse of his brother. In this savage state of mind he passed away on February 9, 1640.

The traveller Evliya Efendi tells us that Murád took much interest in the great mosque of Santa Sophia and worshipped there on Fridays. He erected a wooden enclosure near the southern door in which he placed cages of nightingales and so, in the quaint language of Evliya, 'their sweet notes, mingled with the sound of the Mu'adhdhin's voices, filled the mosque with a harmony approaching that of Paradise.'[1]

The next twelve Sulṭáns until we come to Maḥmúd II (1808) were rulers of no weight or power. They were now brought up in the harems, and Turkey owed whatever vitality she possessed in those years to the vigour and ability of the Viziers. The Khalífa of Islám was a negligable quantity altogether. Of these Sulṭáns, four were deposed, one was assassinated and one resigned. Instead of describing the events in the reign of each of these incompetent rulers I shall take a rapid survey of the principal political events until the accession of Maḥmúd II in 1808.

During part of this period, if Sulṭáns were weak, many of the Viziers were strong men. Muḥammad Kuprili, an Albanian, who received that office in

[1] *Travels of Evliya* (London, 1846), p. 48.

1656 reorganized the fleet, recovered many islands which Venice had seized, and did much to arrest temporarily the decline of the empire. He was a strong and resolute man; armed with absolute power, he could brook no opposition. He is said to have executed thirty-six thousand persons during his five years term of office. He was succeeded by Koprili-zada Aḥmad, an equally strong and able man, who maintained control over the provinces and, though defeated in a war against Austria, was able to conclude an advantageous treaty of peace (1664). He also subdued the island of Crete. These advantages were somewhat lessened by the brilliant victory won by John Sobieski, King of Poland, over the Turks at Lemberg in 1675. This town, recently captured by the Russians, was the most northerly point of the Turkish advance in Europe.

The Cossacks of the Ukraine now began to assert their independence and applied to Russia for aid, the result of which was that Russia now received a cession of territory by a treaty made in 1681, the first of many to follow, all tending to weaken the Turkish empire.

The Reformation had taken deep root in Hungary, but was opposed by the Austrian government, which led on by the Jesuits initiated cruel persecutions against the Protestants. The Magyars, who had embraced the reformed faith, resented this and revolted. The Austrians who were Romanists punished them with great severity. It so happened that at this time the grand Vizier, Kara Muṣṭafá, was a very ambitious man who could brook no opposition,[1] and who saw in the civil war a grand opportunity for gaining Hungary and curbing the power of the House of Hapsburg. Whilst the Turkish empire sorely needed repose and reform, it was a foolish thing to enter upon a great war; but nothing could turn the Vizier from the desire to immortalize his name with a great victory, and so Sulṭán Muḥammad IV and the Vizier in the spring of 1683 set forth with an army of 400,000 men. It was the most determined attempt the Turks had ever made to crush the Christian nations. The army marched towards Vienna and commenced (July 14, 1683), the siege which has become so memorable for its brilliant relief. The fortifications of the city were in a bad state of repair and the prospects of a sound defence were so poor that the Emperor and his Court fled to Bavaria, and had the grand Vizier hastened on, instead of wasting time by devastating the country through which he passed, he might have easily captured the city. The delay was made good use of by the people of Vienna, for the whole population worked hard at the defences and, as a precautionary measure, destroyed all houses in the suburbs.

[1] He reduced the corps of Janissaries to 17,000 men, but it soon rose again to 50,000.

Though the emperor showed himself to be a coward and ran away, there was a brave man left. Count Stahremberg was a true hero and took charge of the defence. For two months the siege was pressed with vigour, but each assault was bravely repulsed and mines were met by counter mines; still the little band of 20,000 combatants could not hold out much longer. Their distressed condition has been thus described :—

> The assaults so far had indeed been fruitless, for the Turkish scimitar was no match for the German halberd, sythe and battle-axe; but the mines were creeping toward the walls and sickness was raging in the city. To sickness followed famine. Cats were so valuable that a chase after the animal over the roofs became a recognized form of sport. The relieving army was known to be on the move, but would it come in time, or would it succeed in driving away the still immense, though diminishing, hosts of the Turks? [1]

John Sobieski, king of Poland, had bound himself by a treaty to assist the emperor Leopold of Austria and both confirmed it by an oath, sworn before the Pope's Legate. They, however, remembered that the Pope claimed a dispensing power (*ante* p. 30) and so they added a clause to the treaty which stated that 'it was not subject to retraction by Papal dispensation'. Sobieski's army 85,000 strong came up fresh and vigorous, and on September 12 completely defeated the Turkish

[1] S. Lane-Poole, *Turkey*, p. 231.

forces. The king's stirring address to the Polish soldiers was:—

Warriors and friends! Yonder in the plains are our enemies. We have to fight them on a foreign soil, but we fight for our own country, and under the walls of Vienna we are defending those of Warsaw and Cracow. We have to save to-day, not a single city, but the whole of Christendom, of which the city of Vienna is the bulwark. The war is a holy one. There is a blessing on our arms, and a crown of glory for him who falls. You fight not for your earthly sovereign, but for the King of Kings . . . I have but one command to give. Follow me! The time is come for the young to win their spurs.[1]

The Grand Vizier prepared for the fight by slaughtering thirty thousand captives. This haughty cruel man was no general. He could slay helpless prisoners but was unable to lead men to victory. The defeat was complete. Three hundred guns and a vast qunatity of war material were captured, the Janissaries were destroyed, and the army was utterly routed. Kara Muṣṭafá incurred the displeasure of his employer, and it is not perhaps to be regretted that he paid with his life for his foolish ambition and barbaric cruelty.

Vienna was, therefore, saved by the patient endurance and heroism of its defenders, by the skilful strategy of John Sobieski and the martial bravery of the relieving force. This was the last great effort made by the Turks to gain more ground in Europe and it failed. They never recovered from the blow,

[1] S. Lane-Poole, *Turkey*, p. 247.

and it now became possible for Hungary, so long the scence of continual wars, to regain her liberty. A few years after, the troops mutinied, dethroned Muḥammad IV and placed his brother Suleymán II (1687–91) on the throne.

From this time onward the gradual decline of the empire is shown by the various treaties made with foreign nations. The treaty of Carlowitz in 1699 took away from Turkey a good part of her Hungarian possessions; and Transylvania went to Austria. There were other adjustments of territory with Poland and Russia. Nineteen years later the remaining provinces in Hungary were given up and Turkish rule there ceased as entirely as that of the Moors in Spain had done in the fifteenth century. In the latter case the Moors left behind memorials of civilization, industry and art which added some glory to their rule; in Hungary the memorials of Turkish occupation were ruin and devastation. They left nothing to add any relief to the sad picture of the misery they had caused.

The treaty of Carlowitz is an important event for it marks the end of Turkey's power as a military nation for offensive purposes in Europe. She was no longer a standing menace to her neighbours in the north. It was also the first occasion on which the representatives of other Powers had taken any part in peace negotiations. Von Hammer says of this treaty :—

It marks the period when men ceased to dread the Ottoman empire as an aggressive power; it was then that the Porte and Russia took part, for the first time, in a general European congress; and by admitting the representatives of England and Holland, neither of which states was a party to the war, both the Sulṭán and the Czar admitted the principle of the intervention of the European Powers, one with another, for the sake of the general good.[1]

An attempt to use the interval of peace for the promotion of internal reforms raised up much opposition and the Sulṭán, Muṣṭafá II, was deposed.

The Russians were now a growing power and their wars, alliances and treaties with Turkey now became constant. Charles XII of Sweden, after his defeat at Pultowa (1709), took refuge in Turkey, and the Sulṭán Aḥmad III had the courage to refuse to give him up to Peter the Great. This led to a war with Russia. According to the custom, now discontinued, on the declaration of war the Turks imprisoned the Russian ambassador in the Castle of the Seven Towers.

The Turks gained the initial advantage on the banks of the river Pruth, and Peter found himself in a precarious position; but the empress Catherine bribed the Grand Vizier and saved the position. The treaty of the Pruth in 1711 and that of Constantinople in 1720 gave Russia some advantage and accession of territory. Soon after this seven

[1] *Geschichte Osmanischen Reiches*, vol. iii, p. 913.

provinces taken from Persia by Murád IV were recovered by Nádir Kulí Khán who in 1736 compelled the successor of Aḥmad III, the Sulṭán Maḥmúd I, to recognize him as the Sháh of Persia.

The reign of Aḥmad III, compared with that of many of his successors was not inglorious. He improved the finances, and though he lost some territory he also gained some. He was a liberal patron of literature and art. During his reign the first printing press was set up in Constantinople.

In 1736 another war broke out and Russia invaded the Crimea. Austria joined in and invaded Bosnia, Serbia and Wallachia, all Turkish provinces. The war was concluded by the treaty of Belgrade in 1739, by which that city was given up by Austria and generally the Turks had the best of the bargain; and it seemed as if evil days might be long deferred.

Later on trouble arose on account of the aggressive policy of Russia in the neighbourhood of the Caspian and the Black Seas and her interference in the affairs of Poland, which led to its partition in 1772. The patriotic Poles appealed to the Sulṭán for aid. This caused much anxiety in Constantinople. In 1768 war was declared and the Russian representative at the Porte was imprisoned. The war went on for some years and was unfavourable to the Turks. Under the weak 'Abdu'l-Ḥamíd I (1773–89) matters grew worse. He had been confined by his brother Sulṭán Muṣṭafá III in the harem for forty-three years, and now passed from the monotony of a royal prison to the care and anxieties of the throne. Naturally he proved to be an incapable ruler. The financial position of the empire was bad and the troops did not receive the large donations usually given to them on the accession of a new sovereign; consequently they became demoralized. Under these circumstances the Turks were compelled to accept the terms laid down in the treaty of Kaynarji in 1774. No previous Sulṭán had ever been asked to accept such onerous terms, and this treaty shows how great a step had been taken towards the dissolution of the Ottoman empire. By it the Crimea was declared independent under its own Khán. Moldavia and Wallachia were restored to Turkey, but, as they were now formally under the protection of Russia, they were practically semi-independent states. Greek traders were permitted to sail under the protection of the Russian flag, which was an important step in the development of the spirit of independence now arising in that long subjugated land.[1] Turkey also had to pay a large war indemnity and by article vii of the treaty the Sublime Porte undertook 'to protect the

[1] For other commercial results which followed from this treaty, see Odysseus, *Turkey in Europe*, pp. 312-3; and for its general terms, see Creasy, *History of the Ottoman Turks*, vol. ii, pp. 257-62.

Christian religion and its churches' and conceded to the Minister of Russia the specific right to 'make representations in favour of the new church', which under article xiv of the same treaty, the Russian government was empowered to build. 'This article is of great historical importance, as forming the basis of the later claim of Russia to possess by treaty the right to protect the orthodox subjects of the Porte.'[1]

A grandson of the empress Catherine was named Constantine, and on a gate in Moscow the words 'The way to Constantinople' were written. These things indicated the policy of Russia which soon began to take a practical turn. In 1779 a Russian nominee was accepted as Khán of the Crimea and in 1783 Russia annexed that province and has retained it ever since. In 1786 Catherine made a triumphal progress in the Crimea.

All this roused the Turks to action, and in 1788 war was again declared and was conducted with very much savagery on both sides. The Russian successes so affeted Sulṭán 'Abdu'l-Ḥamíd I that he died.

His successor, Salím III (1789–1807), wished to carry on the war more strenuously but, as his generals were incompetent and his troops in bad humour, disaster after disaster followed. Further

[1] *Encyclopædia Britannica* (ed. xi), vol. xxvi, p. 454.

opposition was useless and the treaty of Jassy was signed in 1792, by which the river Dniester was made the frontier in Europe and Belgrade was restored to the Turks.

This peace did not, however, restore order in the Turkish empire, and so great was the disorganization that the Serbs saw in it an opportunity for regaining some of their lost liberty. The Dahias, or four chieftains of the Janissaries, had rebelled against the Sulṭán and established themselves in Serbia, where they did as they pleased and oppressed the people.[1] The Serbs in 1804 elected George Petrovitch, better known as Káráġeorge (Black George),[2] commander-in-chief. He had passed an adventurous youth as a soldier, and as a leader of brigands. He was a man of simple habits of life, bold and brave, just suited to the work in hand.[3] The Dahias were defeated and beheaded. The Sulṭán now hoped that Serbia would remain loyal to him, but the Turks were soon driven out of the country and in 1807 the Sultán offered to grant Serbia self-government with Kárágeorge as ruler; but Serbia declined all terms and allied itself with

[1] For a good account of these men, see Miller, *The Balkan States*, pp. 308–9.

[2] He received the nicknames of Tsrni Dyordye from the Serbs, and of Káráġeorge from the Turks, on account of his dark complexion and his gloomy, taciturn temper and disposition.

[3] See Miller, *The Balkan States*, pp. 311-2.

Russia in war upon Turkey. Russia hastily made the treaty of Bucharest (1812), but entirely failed to secure proper terms for Serbia, her faithful ally. The Turks were now set free, and, on the refusal of the Serbs to lay down their arms as a preliminary of peace, they invaded Serbia. Kárágeorge and most of the leading men found safety in flight to Hungary. Two years after the Serbs under Milosh Obronovitch rose in rebellion and so far succeeded that in 1817 Serbia regained its autonomy under the suzerainty of the Sulṭán, and Milosh was declared hereditary prince of the country. In 1817 Kárágeorge suddenly returned to Serbia. Whether he hoped to again place himself at the head of affairs, or was sent by the Greeks to stir up Serbia to a war with Turkey is not known. Anyhow the Turkish Pasha at Belgrade demanded that he should be delivered up. He was murdered in his sleep and his head was sent to Belgrade for transmission to Constantinople. He was ruthless in many ways, but few men could have led undisplined and badly-armed peasants to victory as he did. He is one of the national heroes of the Serbs, a fact which they recognized in 1842 by appointing his son, Alexander, as Prince of Serbia and in 1903 his grandson, Peter Kárágeorgevich, to the same dignity. The autonomy granted in 1817 was confirmed by the treaty of Adrianople in 1839. It was not, however, until 1867 that all the Turkish garrisons were withdrawn. By the treaty of Berlin (1878) Serbia became an independent kingdom, after long centuries of servitude. Since then the Serbs have made great progress and have won renown as bold and successful warriors.

After this digression we must now return to affairs in Turkey. Salím III soon saw that administrative reforms were most urgently called for, and that an improved army system was absolutely needed. Everywhere disorder prevailed. The local governors oppressed the people and did as they pleased. They opposed all attempts at reform. The Sulṭán formed a new body of troops, called the Nizám-i-Jedid, properly drilled and trained. Military schools under European instructors were established and the navy was improved. The Janissaries objected to the whole scheme and supported the officials in their opposition to reforms, both civil and military. They demanded the abolition of the new troops and their combined influence was strong enough to enable them to dethrone the Sulṭán and to proclaim his nephew as the new ruler under the title of Muṣṭafá IV (1807–8).

Meanwhile there were troubles in Serbia due to the lawless conduct of the Janissaries. As we have seen the Serbs under Kárágeorge, rose in rebellion defeated the Janissaries and captured Belgrade. Muṣṭafá IV was not strong enough to carry out his father's plans. The reforms which had been made were abolished, and all who had been concerned in them had to flee from the fury of the Janissaries. The Pasha of Rustchuk responded to the call of the men who had been in sympathy with Salím's plans and marched on Constantinople in order to restore Salím; but before he could reach that city Salím had been killed and Muṣṭafá put to death.

Maḥmúd II (1808–39) was in many ways a strong though despotic ruler. He came to the throne at a period of great unrest, and, though his methods are open to much criticism, it must be admitted that he tried to introduce some reforms into the administration. The decadence of the Ottoman empire had now reached an acute stage. The central power was weak, the provinces were in revolt, the Janissaries could not be controlled, and some of the great Pashas were practically independent rulers. Until now the subject races, though restive and ready at times to help the enemies of the empire, had never risen to achieve their own independence. They had been crushed by centuries of despotism, and weakened by the tribute of their children for the corps of the Janissaries. This had now ceased and, as the flower of provincial youth grew up into manhood, and retained their religion and their national aspirations, the weakness and submissiveness of the people in the country districts passed away, and a new spirit came upon the subject races so long cowed and oppressed. Some of the peoples in the remote and mountainous regions had never really been conquered. The brave Montenegrins were an example of what a small but bold community could do. All this showed the Sulṭán that he must grasp the reins of government more firmly. This he proceeded to attempt.

The Sulṭán, feeling that his control over the great Pashas was insufficient, now determined upon a policy of centralization. In order to do this, it was necessary to reduce the power of the local governors who, in many cases, were practically independent of the central government of Constantinople. The Derebeys held their lands on a feudal tenure and defied the Sulṭán's authority. They were often guilty of extortion from the people over whom they ruled, but still they were men who came from the local families, and they accepted the position of protectors of the people from outside rapacity. It is doubtful whether the rule of officials sent from Constantinople, who often paid large sums for their appointments, was any real improvement in administration, or any greater benefit to the people. If the Derebeys exacted money, they spent it in the locality, and the province as a whole became no poorer. The peasant, when in want, found a chief willing to assist him and so Bey and peasant got along fairly well. Maḥmúd changed all this, resumed the fiefs his predecessors had granted and so destroyed the landed gentry. Possibly it was desirable to exercise more central control, but the change needed to be brought about gradually and cautiously.

One of the greatest of these governors was 'Alí Pasha of Janina, who was practically independent in Albania and paid little attention to orders from Constantinople, and yet he kept his district in order and the Greeks quiet. He was slain in 1820. The people liked their local rulers and did not approve of the corrupt officials sent from Constantinople. If they were to be fleeced, they preferred that men whom they knew should do it—men who would take care that no one else should injure them.

Maḥmúd also realized that he must introduce reforms into the military administration and become independent of the Janissaries, now nominally a force of 135,000 men. In 1825 he formed a body of regular troops called the Eshkenjis, and procured from the Shaikhu'l-Islám a fatvá to the effect that it was quite lawful, and indeed a duty, for Muslims to accept military service. The Janissaries, jealous of their position and power, rose in revolt; but Maḥmúd was prepared for it. For years he had been maturing his plans and in 1826 he struck the blow. The rebellious troops met in the At-Maidan, overturned the caldrons of the various regiments, a signal of rebellion, attacked the house of their Aga, who had agreed to the formation of the new troops, and set about pillaging the city. The 'Ulamá' had stated that it was lawful to oppose and slay violent men, so the law was on the side of the Sulṭán. War was declared and the sacred standard of the Prophet was unfurled; but a more effective step was the presence of the large body of troops, supported by artillery, which marched to the At-Maidan. The Janissaries were asked to lay down their arms. This they refused to do. The order to fire was then given to the artillery gunners, the barracks of the Janissaries were set on fire and large numbers were slain. Of the few who survived the conflict some were afterwards executed, and others were sent to the galleys. Thus perished this famous corps which had won in earlier days so many victories for the Ottoman arms; but had now degenerated into an idle turbulent mob. When the Janissaries had been thus disposed of, the new army on the European model was formed, in the training and disciplining of which the Sulṭán himself took a practical part. Still the loss of an old army before a new one came into efficient being was a danger, for trouble was at hand.

The Greek agitation for freedom now assumed larger proportions. It was no new idea. As far back as 1780 the Society of Friends (Ἑταιρία τῶν φιλικῶν) had been formed and pursued its proselytizing course. Other literary and patriotic societies came into existence. There was a great revival of literary activity and Greek schools were founded in large numbers. The Hetairia now became a real source of danger and the suppression of 'Alí Pasha made its work easier. The Greek insurrection had broken out in 1821 but was put down with much severity.[1] The Patriarch, Gregorius, was executed. This was a wanton and foolish act of revenge. It was deeply resented in Russia, whose ambassador was recalled. The Greek question caused much trouble to the leading European Powers and gave rise to many diplomatic conversations. Then in 1825 England recognized Greece as a belligerent state; whereupon Russia, fearing she might lose her position as a champion of the Greeks, suggested a joint intervention of the Powers. This came to nothing. The Sulṭán then determined to make a supreme effort to subdue the rebellion. He sent to Egypt and called in the aid of Muḥammad 'Alí, Governor of Egypt, who, as the reward for his services, was to receive the island of Crete and the control over Damascus and Syria. The result was the complete conquest of Greece, the occupation of Athens, and the deportation to Cairo of two thousand Greek captives as slaves. This roused considerable feeling against the Turks, but before anything effective was done, Russia had her own grievances to settle. The Porte resented all this outburst of feeling and interference, but was too weak to resist

[1] For a full account of this insurrection, see *The Encyclopædia Britannica* (ed. xi), vol. xii, pp. 493–5.

the demands made upon her. The new army was not ready and so the Sulṭán was obliged to agree to the treaty of Akkerman (1826) in which, amongst other things, the autonomy of Serbia was recognized.

In the political world further steps were then taken with regard to Greece, and the Russian susceptibilities were mollified by a request from Great Britain to join in mutual representations to the Porte. Austria and Prussia objected to any pressure being brought to bear upon the Sulṭán and so the treaty of London (1827) was signed only by Russia, Great Britain and France. The object of the treaty was to secure the autonomy of Greece under the suzerainty of the Sulṭán. Pending the settlement of the question Greece accepted an armistice, but Ibráhím Pasha, the Egyptian commander, declined to do so without orders from the Sulṭán. However, he agreed to detain his ships in the harbour at Navarino. Ibráhím having heard that some Greeks had attacked Turkish ships set sail, but was met by the allied fleets and compelled to return. An accidental encounter led to a general naval battle and to the entire destruction of the Turkish and Egyptian fleets at Navarino on October 20, 1827. The Egyptian army was expelled from the Morea. The Sulṭán was naturally deeply incensed and a war with Russia ensued (1828–9). It was concluded by the treaty of Adrianople (1829 by which Greece was made a tributary state, governed by a prince selected by the Powers, and the Danubian principalities became practically independent states. On February 3, 1830, a protocol was signed by the terms of which the suzerainty of the Sulṭán was abolished and Greece became an independent kingdom. Victor Berard[1] in an eloquent passage describes how Greece, having survived through long ages in spite of many foes now came to her own again. In the past Persians had invaded and Rome had possessed her. Hordes of barbarians ravaged and the Latins conquered her. Norman soldiers, Turkish janissaries, Arab corsairs, Venetian condottieri succeeded each other, to her loss, and then passed away. Turks, Bulgarians, Austrians had tried but could not destroy the indomitable Grecian spirit which had survived all these centuries of disaster and oppression.

Maḥmúd felt the loss of Greece intensely, but now another calamity was about to happen. Muḥammad 'Alí, Governor of Egypt, the most powerful of all the Sulṭán's vassals determined to claim his independence.[2] He asserted that before a stable government could be established in Egypt, it must be free from the control of Pashas sent from Constantinople. This was sound policy and though there is much

[1] See *La Turquie*, p. 350.

[2] For a good account of the early history of this remarkable man and of his character, see Cameron, *Egypt in the Nineteenth Century*, chapters iv, and xix.

that is blameworthy in the character and actions of Muḥammad 'Alí, he deserves credit for his accurate perception of the needs of the situation and his skill in meeting them. On November 1, 1831, Muḥammad 'Alí invaded Syria. He had been promised the Pashaliks of Syria and Damascus for help rendered in Greece. He now said that he wished to take possession of them. For a time the danger was averted, but in 1839 the Sulṭán could restrain himself no longer, and against the advice of his ministers and of the Powers determined to punish his rebellious vassal. His army suffered a great defeat by an Egyptian army under Ibráhím, a son of Muḥammad 'Alí. The news reached the Sulṭán just before his death. In the treaty of 1841 Muḥammad 'Alí was confirmed in his possessions under the suzerainty of the Sulṭán, and Egypt commenced a new career which resulted in her eventually becoming independent of Turkish control.

Maḥmúd reigned for thirty years, during which time he was involved in many wars and had to give up valuable possessions. Greece, Egypt, Algiers were lost to the empire. The principalities on the Danube were no longer under the Sulṭán's control. Russia gained many advantages, and the interference of the Powers in the affairs of Turkey took a new shape and assumed a more persistent character.

Maḥmúd doubtless made mistakes, but he should be given credit for a worthy attempt to reform the administration. The following comment on his work is sound and judicious :—

Now Sulṭán Maḥmúd possessed in an eminent degree the destructive qualities of a Turk and a Musalmán. Without being bound in his private conduct by the rules of the Qur'án, he was in temper and policy a despot and a Caliph. . . . He is by no means deficient in the natural qualities of judgement and resolution. . . but what is to be expected of a sovereign, who from the time of his accession, has made it the principle of his government to preserve order and power by ruining abruptly, or cutting off invidiously not the turbulent alone and the aspiring officers of the Janissaries, but every distinguished candidate for the honours of the state. His reign of more than thirty years was marked by disastrous wars and compulsory cessions. Greece, Egypt and Algiers escaped from his grasp. On the other hand, when he had crushed the mutinous Janissaries, he introduced a system of reforms—to form a regular army in the place of a fanatical factious militia. . . . It is easy to look back now with a pitying smile over the failures, the broken vows, the paper constitutions, of half a century of Ottoman history, and to wonder why people expected so much of Maḥmúd's reforms, why men hoped for the regeneration of 'the unspeakable Turk'—aye and continued to hope for many years after the reforming Sulṭán had been laid in his grave ; but at the time there was something touching in the strong, ignorant man's struggle against the corruptions of his empire—his blind feeling after the best means to raise his country to the level of a European state. We do not imagine him an ideal reformer, a man of broad views, and the wisdom that comes from ripe study ; his mind was built in a narrow and unbending mould, and he did not dream of such a regeneration of Turkey as Canning afterwards attempted. But he saw the first obvious necessities f government, and he made unhesitatingly in their direction. He knew that a strong ruler upheld by a loyal and disciplined army alone could rescue the empire and stem the tide of corruption and foreign aggrandizement.

It was a brave effort, and the more astonishing since it was made in solitude and isolation. No one prompted Maḥmúd, no one can be pointed out as having prominently and voluntarily assisted him; what help he had he commanded and he rewarded. It was his misfortune as well as his glory to be before his age, to attempt reform, however crude and elementary, at a time when no one understood the necessity or believed in the policy.[1]

'Abdu'l-Mejíd (1839–61), son of the late Sulṭán, succeeded him. Fourteen years of peace followed which allowed time for the further prosecution of the reforms which Maḥmúd had set on foot; but the new Sulṭán, an amiable man, was not strong enough to deal with the difficult position and the many complicated questions which confronted him. Stratford Canning thus sums up his character:—

The graciousness of his manner, and the intelligent, though gentle and even melancholy, expression of his countenance, warrant a hope, perhaps a sanguine one, that with riper years and more experienced judgement he may prove a real blessing and a source of strength to his country. [2]

This sanguine hope was not fulfilled. Still progress in reform was made, but it was due to the untiring energy and tactful determination of the British Ambassador at the Porte, Sir Stratford

[1] S. Lane-Poole, *Life of the Rt. Hon. Stratford Canning* (London, 1888), vol. i, pp. 399–400, 503; vol. ii, pp. 72–3.

[2] Ibid., vol. ii, p. 81.

Canning, who from 1842 occupied a position of supreme importance. He saw that, if Turkey was to be saved, it must be from within and he eagerly supported the men who, like that enlightened statesman Rashíd Pasha, knowing something of western civilization, saw that the old position of isolation and contempt for things new must pass away. Though opposed by the more conservative party in the state, he was yet recognized as a true friend. His personal character was high, his insight keen, his judgement accurate. He rightly earned the title of the Great Elchi (Ambassador). The following statement gives us the key to his success :—

Truthful and straightforward in all his ways, he never condescended to the tricks of diplomacy, and the Turks soon began to perceive that what Canning spoke was the truth. Gifted, moreover, with a sedate gravity which gave dignity and importance to the smallest negotiations—and which was the more valuable because men knew that beneath the calm and polished surface lay an impetuous, passionate spirit, impatient of restraint—the manner of the great Elchi was full of charm and persuasion. . . . The Turkish Ministers and the Sulṭán himself bowed themselves down before his righteous indignation. By force of character, by a certain admirable violence, necessary in dealing with dilatory and prevaricating people, by a kingly grace and courtesy which stamped him as a gentleman of the true sort, but above all by a manly unswerving honesty and straightforwardness, Stratford Canning acquired that extraordinary influence which no Christian has exercised before or since over the princes and statesmen of the Ottoman empire.[1]

Before Canning's return to Constantinople, Rashíd Pasha, however, had persuaded the young Sulṭán, soon after his accession, to promulgate the Tanzímát, or Ḥaṭṭ-i-Sharíf of Gulhané. Its provisions were good—the restraint of the use of arbitrary power by state officials; security for life and property; the equality of subjects of all races and creeds before the law. The latter clause was quite unexpected. The non-Muslim subjects of Turkey had ever been kept in a condition of servitude, protected as tax payers to keep up and support a dominant ruling class. Sulṭán Ibráhím in 1644 had desired to ameliorate their condition, but was opposed by the Shai<u>kh</u>u'l-Islám. Muṣṭafá Kuprili, the able Vizier (1689–91) of Suleymán II did something to improve their position; but the constant wars with Russia, Serbia and other nations stimulated afresh the feeling of resentment towards the Rayas, as the Christian subjects of the Porte are called.

The Tanzímát was premature. It was not favourably received by the ruling class. Rashíd Pasha had to resign his office of Vizier and a strong reaction set in. Then came Stratford Canning, and year in and year out he laboured unceasingly for justice to the Rayas, and against all injustice and corruption in the administration in all

[1] S. Lane-Poole, *Turkey*, pp. 351–2.

departments of the state. After a few years he succeeded in obtaining the re-appointment of Rashíd Pasha, and then he made some progress. His cardinal policy was that there should be equal citizenship for all. This was then a novel doctrine in Turkey, and men were surprised when in 1844 he secured from the Sulṭán a promise that torture should be abolished, obnoxious taxes repealed, and last and greatest of all an order that apostates from Islám to Christianity should not be put to death,[1] and other concessions.

[1] The teaching of the Qur'án on the subject of apostasy is not very clear. There are two verses which may be quoted as having, perhaps, an indirect bearing on the subject. 'For this cause have we ordained to the children of Israel that he who slayeth any one, unless it be a person guilty of slaughter or of spreading disorder in the land, shall be as though he had slain all mankind' [Súratu'l-Má'ida (v) 35]. Apostasy may be brought under 'spreading disorder'. Baiḍáwí explains these words as 'polytheism and idolatry' (الشرك و قطع الطريق). Another verse is: 'As to those who return to their errors after the guidance hath been made plain to them. Satan shall beguile them . . . the angels in causing them to die, shall smite them on the face and back' [Súratu Muḥammad (xlvii) 27, 29]. The immediate reference is to those who were reluctant to follow the standard of the Prophet in his early wars; but Muslim jurists often make such limited judgements of universal application. Still, even then the punishment decreed seems to be in a future life. However, all this matters little, as Muslím law depends on the Sunna as well as on the Qur'án, and the Traditions are clear on the subject. The law as it now stands is that apostates are outlaws, and a person who kills an outlaw would not be liable to punishment under the law of Islám. See Mr. Justice 'Abdu'r-Raḥím, *Muḥammadan Jurisprudence* (Madras, 1911), p. 253.

It was one thing to get an order passed or a promise made and quite another to see the one obeyed or the other kept; but the watchful eye of the Ambassador was ever observant and no official was safe whose misdeeds were brought to his notice. The various proposals for the internal improvement of the administration made by Canning were considered by a Commission which sat at the Porte in 1848. The trouble involved in all this is best told by Canning's biographer:—

> In December, 1848, a Commission sat at the Porte to take into consideration the various proposals which Canning had brought forward for the improvement of the internal administration. In August, 1850, Canning reported that 'nothing had occurred to enliven the prospect'. His advice had been uniform and consistent, but all the fruits were 'delays and evasions, unnecessary compromises, and weak compliances'; corrupt practices in office, a low revenue, high prices, a pernicious system of recruiting the army and a worse one of farming the taxes; discontent in the frontier provinces, and a fanatical spirit towards the Christians, who were massacred in several of the more remote districts; want of inland communications, and a weak state of the military defences—in short an alarming decrepitude in every department of the empire.[1]

Whilst all this was going on two serious political troubles arose. A struggle for liberty in Hungary had been put down with much severity by Austria[2]

[1] S. Lane-Poole, *Life of the Rt. Hon. Stratford Canning*, vol. ii, pp. 207, 210.

[2] See Vanbery, *Hungary*, ch. xv.

and Kossuth and other patriots found refuge in Turkey in 1849. The emperors of Austria and Russia demanded their extradition. The Turks refused to give them up and were supported by Sir Stratford Canning. It seemed as if war was imminent but the appearance of the French and English fleets at the Hellespont had the desired effect and nothing further happened.

The other affair, apparently insignificant in itself, led to more serious consequences. By an arrangement made between Sulṭán Maḥmúd I and Louis XV of France, French pilgrims and those from other Christian nations had been placed under the protection of the king of France. After that time Russia had been persistent in her demands for the pilgrims and clergy of the Orthodox Church. The Latins and the orthodox monks had unseemly quarrels at Jerusalem which they might have been left to settle by themselves; but the emperor Napoleon III, who disliked Russia,[1] made it an opportunity for seeking a quarrel with the Czar, and possibly for gaining the favour of the priests in France. He made demands which were offensive to Russia, and Turkey found it almost impossible to satisfy both parties. A compromise was suggested, but

[1] The emperor Nicholas opposed the first Napoleon's assumption of the title of emperor, and proposed a clause in the treaty of Paris (1814) which would exclude the dynasty of Napoleon from the throne of France. See Skrine, *Russia*, p. 149.

Russia claimed a protectorate over all Turkish subjects who belonged to the Orthodox Church. This could not be granted and so Russia declared war in 1853. England and France in 1854 joined Turkey and the Crimean war began.

It was ended by the treaty of Paris in 1856. By the terms of that treaty Russia abandoned her claim to exercise a protectorate over the Christians in Turkey and to an exclusive right of interference in the Danubian principalities. The contracting Powers agreed to guarantee the integrity and independence of the Ottoman empire. The Sulṭán also reaffirmed in the Ḥaṭṭ-i-Humayún the principles of reform laid down in the Tanzímát of 1839. This new decree—the Ḥaṭṭ-i-Humayún—promising reforms in the administration and better treatment of the Christian subjects was embodied in the treaty of Paris (1856). The Turks, however, are past masters in the art of procrastination and this portion of the treaty has been described as 'brave words and nothing more'.

In this imperial proclamation the Sulṭán announced his desire of renewing and enlarging the numerous improvements which had been introduced into his institutions, with a view to making them worthy of the place which his empire held among civilized nations; he was anxious, he said, to ensure the happiness of his people, who in his sight were all equal, and equally dear to him, and with this object he first confirmed the former guarantees of the Ḥaṭṭ-i-Sharíf of Gulhané to all his subjects, without distinction of class or religion, for their security in person, property and honour; and at the same time renewed all the privileges and spiritual immunities granted *ab antiquo* and subsequently to Christian and other non-Musulman communities established in Turkey. The proclamation went on to enumerate various ecclesiastical privileges, guaranteed the free exercise of its religious rites and the control of its sacred and educational buildings to each and every sect; and made the following announcement in bold terms:—

> Every distinction or designation, tending to make any class whatever of the subjects of my empire inferior to another class on account of their religion, language or race, shall be for ever effaced.[1]

But the treaty of Paris, while recognizing the importance of the measure, specially enacted that the recognition of the Ḥaṭṭ did not entitle any of the Powers, collectively or severally, to interfere in the internal affairs of the Ottoman empire. The qualification abrogated whatever effect the recognition might have had.[2]

Stratford Canning left Constantinople in 1858 and no one else possessed the same influence, or the power of making Turkish ministers realize that the safety of their country depended on internal reforms

[1] S. Lane-Poole, *Life of the Rt. Hon. Stratford Canning*, vol. ii, pp. 440–1.

[2] Ibid., vol. ii, p. 442.

and liberal measures for all classes of their subjects, so still more evil days were to befall the empire.

In June 1861 'Abdu'l-Mejíd was succeeded by his brother 'Abdu'l-'Azíz. Turkey was now admitted into the ranks of the great Powers, and the new Sulṭán, an ignorant and extravagant man, used the position to incur a heavy national debt which brought the country to the verge of bankruptcy.

There were troubles in Serbia owing to the continued presence of Turkish garrisons in that country; but in 1867 they were withdrawn and thus one great step was gained towards full independence. A serious revolt also broke out in Bosnia and Herzegovina in 1875; followed by one in Bulgaria in 1876. These were put down with such severity and barbarity that the sympathies of persons otherwise friendly were alienated. The Sulṭán's extravagance had depleted the treasury, and the strain on it owing to the military measures now taken caused the financial situation to collapse aud Turkey became bankrupt.

Then a conspiracy was formed headed by Midhat Pasha to bring about a change. The Shaikhu'l-Islám issued a fatvá authorizing the deposition of 'Abdu'l-'Azíz.[1] This was done in 1876 and soon after the Sulṭán was found dead, it is said, killed by his own

[1] For a full description of the way in which this was done, see *The Life of Midhat Pasha*, pp. 83-6.

hand. His successor Murád V, a son of 'Abdu'l-Mejíd, reigned three months, when he was deposed as an imbecile. Then on August 31, 1876, 'Abdu'l-Ḥamíd II, a brother of Murád, ascended the throne and reigned until 1909.

The new Sulṭán like his predecessor was unwilling to carry out any practical measure of reform, and as years went on he exhibited a tyrannical spirit and took no pains to suppress the most barbarous treatment of his Christian subjects. At the commencement of his reign, however, he had to make a show of liberality, for soon after his accession a Conference of the Powers met at Constantinople, but its very moderate proposals were rejected by the Sulṭán, who on December 23, 1876, promulgated a constitution which had been prepared by the reforming party.[1] The Sulṭán never had any intention of allowing it to become operative. The formal proclamation

[1] The leader of this party was Midhat Pasha, then Grand Vizier. The new Sulṭán had made promises which raised the hopes of the reformers and now gave his somewhat qualified approval to the new constitution (*see The Life of Midhat Pasha*, pp. 128-30). If he had then followed the advice of his wiser councillors, the revolution which a few years ago led to his deposition might never have occurred. Midhat Pasha was banished soon after and finally tried on the charge of being accessory to the murder of 'Abdu'l-'Azíz though it was generally believed that the Sulṭán committed suicide (op. cit. pp. 90-1). Still Midhat was known to be an opponent of 'Abdu'l-Hamíd's autocratic rule and this charge was found sufficient to lead to his imprisonment and probably, to his subsequent assassination (op. cit. ch. xiii).

of it was a successful attempt to checkmate the Conference and nothing more.

Russia then declared war (April, 1877) which was concluded by the treaty of San Stefano, March 3, 1878. The terms of the treaty were considered to be too harsh and Russia consented to a revision of it and so it was abrogated by the treaty of Berlin, June, 1878. Even this revised treaty was a great blow to Turkey. Serbia, Montenegro and Rumania were formally declared independent. Austria occupied Bosnia and Herzgovina and, after some delays and a great deal of correspondence, Bulgaria was divided into two parts, one autonomous;[1] the other, Eastern Rumelia,[2] in 1885 was added to Bulgaria. In 1885, in response to a popular movement, the two provinces were united, and in 1909 the whole was recognized as an independent state, on the payment of an indemnity for railways and in lieu of the tribute previously paid to the Porte. Greece gained as accession of territory. England was in some ambiguous way pledged to see that reforms were

[1] Writing in 1900 Odysseus says: 'In agriculture, manufactures, commerce, education, literature and military matters they (the Bulgarians) have made enormous strides. It is only necessary to go westward from Turkey and cross the frontier to see what twenty years of autonomy have done.' *Turkey in Europe*, p. 351.

[2] This province remained subject to the authority of the Sulṭán, though it was placed under a Christian governor and an autonomous administration.

carried out, and with this in view took possession of the island of Cyprus, paying to the Sulṭán an annual tribute.[1]

It is true that when peace was restored there was again some talk of reforms and a parliament was summoned; but it was soon dissolved and the constitution was suspended. No further attempts at reform were made, and whatever were the obligations England took upon herself after the treaty of Berlin, she never seems to have fulfilled them. In Armenia the barbarity of the Kurdish soldiers, known as the Ḥamídian cavalry, was so severe that the people rose in revolt, which was put down with great severity and the most horrible massacres, resulting in the death of 200,000 people.

Affairs in Crete also were so mismanaged that Greece began to take action which led to a war with Turkey in 1897. Europe intervened and Turkey gained some accession of territory and a war indemnity; but Crete, though nominally Turkish, was placed under Prince George of Greece, as High Commissioner, approved by the Powers. It has since been ceded to Greece.

The treaty of Berlin had left the Macedonian question in an unsettled condition. The Muslim

[1] Owing to the recent declaration of war with Turkey, by an Order in Council, dated November 3, 1914, Cyprus has been annexed to the British empire and the large annual payment as tribute to the Porte will cease.

and Christian inhabitants suffered from the incompetence and rapacity of the Turkish officials. They saw that the neighbouring states were now free and insurrections broke out. The Powers made various attempts to solve the difficult problems involved, but nothing satisfactory resulted. Thus the reign of 'Abdu'l-Ḥamíd proved a most disastrous one for Turkey. He strove hard to bring about the realization of the Pan-Islámic idea—the union of all Muslims under his leadership as Khalífa; the abolition of the capitulations (*ante* p. 61) and a revocation of all privileges previously granted to non-Muslim subjects of the Porte. He steadily set his face against all reform movements, and surrounded by a palace clique of favourites, centralized all authority in himself and seriously interfered with the administration of his ministers. In order to bring the Kurds under his personal control, he raised fifty-four squadrons of Kurdish nomads and called them the Ḥamídian cavalry. He used them to carry out his pitiless policy with the Armenians. In all this he was supported by his Vizier, Said Pasha, who, however, having offended his master was finally dismissed.

The next Vizier, Kiamil Pasha, was a wise ruler, and for some years the state of affairs improved; but, in due course, the dislike of the Sulṭán to anything like ministerial independence placed such obstacles in the way of the administration of the empire that

Kiamil resigned. Other more subservient ministers were found and the personal autocratic rule of the Sulṭán brought more disasters in its train. By means of his spies, he obtained information about his officials, and no honest independent man had any prospect of permanence in his office. Massacres in Constantinople and in Armenia, revolutions in Yemen and in Crete, troubles with the Druses and in the Balkans arising from unwise control—all these were among the incidents fast bringing Turkey to ruin. As for a government under such conditions, if it had been composed of the most capable statesmen who could have been found in Europe, its action would have been paralysed under such a regime. Every minister had under, or more correctly over, him a subordinate directly nominated by the palace. It was the business of the latter functionary to carry out the views prevailing at Yildiz Kiosk, with or without the approval of his superior, so that frequently, after orders had been sent out by a minister, instructions of a diametrically opposite kind were issued by his lieutenant. Among the offices within the palace the most important was the detective and espionage office. An enormous number of spies were employed. This system, inaugurated by 'Abdu'l-Ḥamíd, was one of the main causes of the unhappy state of the country under his rule. From the encouragement given to secret reports, whether false or true, no one was safe.

The emperor of Germany paid two visits to Constantinople, the second one being in 1898, and the result was the extension of German influence in that city, and also the securing of valuable railway concessions. A proposal that Turkey should join the Triple Alliance was not formally accepted, but the idea was latent and has now been brought into effect, curiously enough not by the followers of 'Abdu'l-Ḥamid, but by his enemies—the Young Turkey party. Then, as now, the wiser Turkish statesmen held aloof. Few Sulṭáns in the past have had the opportunities for good which lay before 'Abdu'l-Ḥamíd at the time of his accession, and few amongst them could have so utterly failed. It was absolutely impossible that things could go on much longer in this hopeless way. A change was needed if the empire was to be saved.

Then came the revolution of 1908, brought about by the Young Turkey party. The revolt began on July 22, 1908, and on the following day in Salonica the Committee of Union and Progress proclaimed a new constitution. Two days after this the Sulṭán much against his will agreed to restore the constitution proposed by Midhat Pasha in 1876, and ordered the election of a Chamber of Deputies. Austria now became alarmed lest a reformed Turkey might require her to evacuate Bosnia and Herzegovina which she had occupied after the Berlin Congress in 1878. The matter was finally arranged by Austria annexing these two states and by the payment to Turkey of £2,200,000 as compensation for the Turkish crown lands taken over in these two countries. How long the Bosnians will remain under alien Austrian rule, when they see the marvellous progress, which the other Slav states, now free, are making, is very doubtful. The result of the present (1914) great European war will probably lead to the transfer of these provinces to Serbia and Montenegro.

A counter revolution, connived at by the Sulṭán, was organized, but the army under Enver Bey marched to Constantinople, deposed 'Abdu'l-Ḥamid, in 1909, and appointed in his place his brother under the title of Muḥammad V. Little is known of the new Sulṭán to whom no power is given. 'Abdu'l-Ḥamíd is now confined as a state prisoner and has time to reflect on his many crimes and cruelties.

The advent of the Young Turkey party was hailed with much satisfaction by all the friends of Turkey. They saw in the proposed liberal institutions and promised reforms a prospect for the revival of the Ottoman empire. A prominent European statesmen spoke of the movement as having but one end—the welfare of all Turkish subjects, and the orderly establishment of constitutional rule. The most recent events, however, show that such sanguine hopes were premature, for it is this very party, rash, misguided and foolish, which has brought Turkey nearer to utter ruin than even the worst of her Sulṭáns has ever done.

The difficulties before the Young Turks were very great. They had to contend against the conservative religious spirit, which is not favourable to progressive ideas. Islám does not easily lend itself to essential modifications. These men, educated in Berlin and Paris, were looked upon as lax Muslims. Whether that was so or not, the suspicion was current and operative. Nationality and liberty (watan and hurriyat) were the watchwords of the new party; but the old Turk thinks less of the nation than of the religion and less of freedom than of submission. His glory is that he esteems Islám above all else and that as a Muslim he is greater than as a Turk. In addition to this there was the political position. In Arabia, Syria and Macedonia there was much popular discontent requiring strong but sympathetic treatment, for their grievances were very real. Every branch of the administration required re-organization and large sums of money before any one of them could be made even moderately efficient. The law had been codified, but was administered by men paid so badly that bribery was almost a necessity to them. Everywhere roads, bridges and public works were needed and the treasury was empty. The relations of Turkey with the great Powers called for much political sagacity and this quality, as regards foreign affairs, does not seem to have been prominent amongst the leaders in the Committee of Union and Progress—that extraordinary power behind the throne, which compelled the government of the day to carry out the wishes of the Young Turks. In the place of the personal despotism of 'Abdu'l-Ḥamíd we find the corporate despotism of a Committee, the constitution of which is known only to a few. One of the chief military leaders, Enver Bey, was educated in Berlin and is said to have married a German lady. Whether led by him or not, the fact remains that the Young Turks looked more to Germany than to the old friends of Turkey, England and France. They were annoyed because the Powers of the Triple Entente exercised some protection over Crete, and this was one among several causes which turned them towards the Triple Alliance. The history of the past should have shown them the unwisdom of taking sides in European politics, but the Turk has always found it hard to learn a lesson and has suffered in consequence. One result of this change of attitude was that France, hitherto the banker of Turkey, declined to lend more money.

Turkey is composed of many races, speaking many languages and professing various forms of religion. To rule equitably such a variety of races requires statesmanship of a high order, and an administration which will safeguard the rights of each community and allow each to develop on its own lines. The Young Turks made a mistake in attempting to make Turkish the official language to be used in all departments, including that of public instruction throughout the empire. This at once raised up opposition in Syria where Arabic is the mother tongue and is looked upon by the Muslims there as a sacred language. The efforts made to substitute the Arabic character in which Turkish is written for the national ones in writing the various languages of the Turkish Balkan provinces was a mistake. It roused the national spirit in people longing to be free. It thus became perfectly clear that the new goverment meant to Ottomanise the whole country. Thus it is said:—

> They wish Albanians, Armenians, Jews, Greeks, Arabs, Syrians, Kurds, and all the nationalities of Macedonia, to sink their respective national individualities into one single nationality—which shall have for its principal element the Young Turk himself—for choice speaking the Turkish language, and using the Arabic alphabet, the only form of writing in which the Turkish language is ever expressed. In this way alone do they perceive the possibility of making Turkey strong and powerful. And as they are at the present moment in control of the army through which the revolution was effected, they propose to use force to accomplish this purpose. Turkey once united, and her army reorgaized, then let those Balkan states which have been broken piecemeal from the Ottoman empire have a care. Let everybody have a care, for the Turk will then be as good as anybody else in Europe or Asia.[1]

[1] Dr. Fraser, *Persia and Turkey in Revolt*, p. 433.

If the Turk had been popular that might have been done; but he is hated by the Muslim Arabs and mistrusted by the Christian rayas. The Young Turks were in this matter idealists, with a vision of one great united Ottoman community, in which Ottoman language, law, custom and policy should exist supreme. This showed serious lack of statesmanship and want of administrative experience. It brought its punishment, for this attempt to crush out national feelings and aspirations in the Balkans was the main cause of the recent Balkan war, so disastrous to Turkey.

Great attention was paid to the army, which was largely trained by German officers; but the lack of a supply of intelligent junior officers and incompetence in other departments connected with the army led to its defeat in the first great war it undertook. Still, after all, the Young Turks kept the state going, which considering how corrupt it had been under 'Abdu'l-Ḥamíd was not an easy thing to do.

In November, 1911, Italy annexed Tripoli. Turkey refused to recognize this action and war was declared between the two countries. By the treaty of Lausanne, October, 1912, Turkey granted autonomy to Tripoli without officially recognising Italy's sovereignty. This curious method of saving the face of the Khalífa is shown in the following terms of the treaty:—

(i) Italy maintains absolutely the law which declared her full and entire sovereignty over Lybia, and, in consequence, denies any form of sovereignty there on the part of Turkey, whether open or disguised, nominal, effective, or partial. Nor does she consent to such sovereignty under the form of a territorial concession made to Turkey.

(ii) Turkey, on her side, neither impugns nor recognizes the sovereignty of Italy. She ignores it; and in that manner avoids offending against the letter of the Coran law which forbids the cession of lands of the Caliph to the infidel. Italy consents to forego the formal recognition by Turkey, and will be content with procuring a recognition of her new rights from the Powers.

It will be seen that the Sulṭán simply ignores the cession of territory. Italy accepts the position and does not demand any formal recognition of the occupation of Tripoli. All parties understand that Tripoli now belongs to Italy; but the face of the K͟halífa had to be saved and this is the curious way of doing it.

In August, 1912, a massacre at Kotchana led to a strong protest from Bulgaria. The Balkan states—Bulgaria and Serbia—formed an alliance with Greece and required Turkey to carry out the long-promised and long-desired reforms in Macedonia. Turkey refused to do so and war broke out on October 8, 1912. By the treaty of London, May 30, 1913, many Turkish provinces passed to the allies, and the Ottoman possessions in Europe now consist only of Constantinople and the vilayet of Adrianople.

All her African possessions had been previouly lost. The empire in Asia is still extensive and under good government might be made highly prosperous; but the records of the history of the Ottoman Turks for many past centuries affords little hope of such a result.

When the whole civilized world was struck with great horror at the barbarities of 'Abdu'l-Ḥamíd, the Kaiser, for purely political purposes, condoned his brutalities, was his guest for four days, went out of his way to flatter him and thereby gained certain concessions, notably those in connexion with the Baghdad railway;[1] and now strange to say Germany retains her influence with the Turkish enemies of 'Abdu'l-Ḥamíd. The result is that Turkey finds it difficult to get loans from France, except upon the most stringent conditions. France is therefore looked upon with disfavour; but France has no desire to find funds for Germans in Turkey to spend. England is the ally of France and so all her past good deeds are forgotten, British enterprises are treated with hostility, and no effort is made to retain even her regard. Germany has now more than recovered the position she held in 'Abdu'l-Ḥamíd's time, and has drawn, at least, the Young Turkey Party towards the Triple Alliance. Austria practically stole the provinces of Bosnia and Herzegovina, but even that

[1] For an excellent account of this concession, see, Valentine Chirol, *The Middle Eastern Question*, chapters xviii, xix, xx.

offence is now condoned by the Young Turks, as she is the ally of Germany.

In the history of the Muslim world chauvinism has played a great part. The chauvinism of the Arabs ruined the Umayyad Khalífate; it worked evil in Muslim Spain;[1] and now it is apparent in the Turkish army under the control of the Committee of Union and Progress. The influence of Germany has stimulated this spirit of chauvinism, of which she possesses so large a share; it has encouraged amongst the Young Turks an arrogant militarism which seeks to control the political destinies of the country. Thus gradually the gulf has widened between Turkey and her real friends—nations which in the Crimean war spent millions of money and gave up the lives of thousands of their heroic sons for the safety of Turkey; all this and many other kindly deeds are forgotten and Turkey, controlled by the Germanized military party, ranges itself on the side of the common enemies of her benefactors.

Thus, at last, unless the more sober-minded leaders, the real statesmen in Turkey, and the Sulṭán himself can control Enver Bey and his associates, now completely hypnotized by German wiles, the decay of Turkey, which has been going on as we have seen for centuries, will proceed at an accelerated pace.

[1] See Sell, *Muslim Conquests in Spain* (C.L.S.), p. 6.

On June 28, 1914, the Archduke Franz Ferdinand, the heir to the throne of Austria-Hungary, and his wife were assassinated at Sarajevo in Bosnia. The Government of Austria-Hungary presented a note to Serbia on July 23, alleging that these murders were caused, or at least encouraged, by Serbian officers and officials. This note made demands on Serbia which no self-respecting independent kingdom could concede, and required a reply within forty-eight hours. Serbia replied conceding most of the Austrian demands, but objecting to some of the most extreme among them; whereupon on July 28 Austria-Hungary declared war on Serbia. Russia then mobilized a part of its army, and immediately Germany also mobilized and invaded French territory and declared war on Russia. On August 4, Germany violated the neutrality of Belgium which she had signed a treaty to protect, and Great Britain, after twelve hours' notice, declared war on Germany.

Soon after the war began, two German warships, the *Goeben* and *Breslau*, in order to avoid capture entered the Straits of the Dardenelles. According to international law, the Ottoman Government should have ordered them to go out of neutral waters within a reasonable time and, if they failed to do so, should have dismantled and interned them until the close of the war; after which they would have been returned to Germany. The Turkish

Government did nothing of the kind, but, on the pretence that it had purchased the ships from Germany, retained the German officers and crew in its own naval service. It further imported a large number of mechanics and quantities of warlike stores from Germany. The British naval instructors in the service of the Porte were superseded, and the whole naval administration passed into the hands of German officers, under the supreme control of Enver Bey, the Minister for War who, a Pole by extraction and a German by sympathy,[1] was the leader of the Turkish pro-German party. The British Government protested against this breach of neutrality, and the Grand Vizier again and again said that the Germans would be dismissed. There seems to be some reason to suppose that he was really anxious to avoid a rupture with Great Britain, but it is equally clear that the masterful spirit of Enver Bey dominated the government and that neither the Grand Vizier, nor the Minister of the Interior, nor even the Sulṭán himself, could withstand the imperious demands of the Minister for War and the Germans in Constantinople, who had practically become the dominant rulers of the city.

The war party proceeded to mobilize troops, to prepare for the invasion of Egypt, to bribe the Bedawín to warlike action, and to demand the

[1] Dillon, *A Scrap of Paper*, p. 68.

departure of British ships from Mohammerah, a Persian port over which the Turks had no authority. All the time the Grand Vizier protested that he desired peace and made many excuses about the delay in dismissing the officers and crews of the German ships. Then followed the detention of British merchant ships in Turkish waters, attempts to stir up disaffection in Persia, India, Egypt, and amongst the Sanúsís in Africa, violent attacks in Turkish newspapers, now subsidized by German gold, against England declaring that she was the enemy of Islám ; the abolition of the capitulations and the closing of foreign post offices, and numberless other acts of a highly provocative character.

The British Government was most patient and waited week after week for the dismissal of the Germans. It even, whilst protesting that the abolition of the capitulations, which were based on many ancient treaties, and could only be set aside by mutual consent, expressed its willingness, if the German officers and crews of the *Goeben* and *Breslau* were dismissed, to consider, with the allied Powers, the question of the capitulations, and with them to come to some arrangement and to withdraw their extra territorial jurisdiction, as soon as a scheme of judicial administration which would satisfy modern conditions was set up.

The subsidized Turkish papers gave the most misleading information, supplied from German sources, about the progress of the war. People were led to believe that victory was certain to the Germans; which statements, combined with inflammatory articles against England, helped to draw the more thoughtless Turks to the side of Enver Bey and the war party. It was even said that the Kaiser had become a Muslim and was fighting for Islám against Russia.

It soon became clear that, notwithstanding the Grand Vizier's assurances to the contrary, the *Goeben* and *Breslau*, flying the Turkish flag, but manned by German crews and under the command of German officers, would enter the Black Sea. As a matter of fact, this did take place. Then, on October 29, 1914, Turkish torpedo-boats raided Odessa, sank a Russian gunboat and damaged French and Russian ships. The response to this unwarranted act of hostility was the withdrawal of the Russian Ambassador from Constantinople and the despatch of Sir Edward Grey, British Foreign Minister, to the British Ambassador at Constantinople, of the following instructions:—

SIR EDWARD GREY to SIR L. MALLET

Foreign Office

October 30, 1914

In view of hostile acts that have been committed, the Russian Government have instructed the Russian Ambassador to leave Constantinople with all his staff.

Should His Excellency leave, you should yourself send in a note to the Sublime Porte to say that His Majesty's Government have learnt with the utmost surprise of the wanton attacks made upon open and undefended towns of a friendly country without any warning and without the slightest provocation, and that these acts constitute an unprecedented violation of the most ordinary rules of international law, usage, and comity. Russia has shown the utmost patience and forbearance in face of repeated violations of the rules of neutrality by Turkey, and in face of most provocative acts, amounting in reality to acts of hostility, and in this attitude of restraint her allies, Great Britain and France, have co-operated. It is evident that there is no chance of a return to a proper observance of neutrality so long as the German naval and military missions remain at Constantinople, and such a situation cannot be prolonged.

Unless, therefore, the Turkish Government will divest themselves of all responsibility for these unprovoked acts of hostility by dismissing the German military and naval missions, and fulfilling their often repeated promises about the German crews of the *Goeben* and *Breslau*, and will give you a satisfactory reply to this effect within twelve hours from the date of the delivery of the note, you should ask for your passports and leave Constantinople with the staff of the embassy.

On November 4, Tewfik Pasha, the Turkish Ambassador in London, applied for his passports and a state of war commenced.

A perusal of the White Book [1] from which the above facts are taken shows how patient the British

[1] *Miscellaneous No. 13* (1914) Correspondence Respecting Events leading to the Rupture of Relations with Turkey.

Government was under all the equivocations, delays and hostile actions. Until the very last the Ambassador hoped that the Grand Vizier would be able to control the fiery and ambitious Minister for War. Enver Bey, supported by his German friends, became the real ruler of Turkey. The Sulṭán and his Vizier, assuming that their expressions of a desire for peace were genuine, have proved themselves to be quite powerless. The history of the past shows that the Ottoman Empire prospered only when Sulṭán and Viziers were strong men; when they are weak and helpless disorder and anarchy must follow.

Turkey had received the most complete assurance of British friendship. Sir Edward Grey in his letter of August 18, 1914, states the case to the British Ambassador at the Porte thus:—

> I told the Turkish Ambassador, who had expressed uneasiness as to our intentions towards Turkey, that Turkey would have nothing to fear from us, and that her integrity would be preserved in any conditions of peace which affected the Near East provided that she preserved a real neutrality during the war, made the *Breslau* and *Goeben* entirely Turkish by sending away the German crews of these vessels, and gave all ordinary facilities to British merchant vessels.

The time will come, if it has not already done so, when the more intelligent Turkish people will regret the culpable weakness of their government, for the loss to Turkey will be very great. The attempt of the war party to stir up a Jihád, or Holy War, has utterly failed. Under no possible interpretation of Muḥammadan law could a Jihád in the present circumstances be proclaimed, nor could it possibly be made an obligatory duty (farḍu'l-'ain) on any Muslim to obey such a call to arms. In fact, the conduct of the Turkish Government has been condemned by all responsible rulers throughout the Islámic world, and the Muslim soldiers of Russia, France and England are fighting loyally and valiantly in defence of their respective empires. They, at least, have no desire to come under the despotic rule of the German military party, or to aid Turkey in her folly in so doing. It is a sad sight to good Muslims to see their Khalífa thus helpless in the hands of unwise and unpatriotic advisers.

One of the first results of the present war was that Egypt, which from the time of Salím, has been ruled by Turkey or has been under her suzerainty, became free from all Turkish control real or imaginary. We have seen how Muḥammad 'Alí became Viceroy of Egypt (*ante* p. 90), though compelled to pay a large annual tribute as a sign of the Sulṭán's suzerainty. In January, 1863, Ismá'íl Pasha became Viceroy. He was an ambitious man and sought to weaken the ties which still bound Egypt to Turkey. The Sulṭán 'Abdu'l-'Azíz paid a visit to Cairo and as the result of the conferences then held, and aided by large bribes to the Grand Vizier, the Porte allowed the title of Khedive to be substituted for that of Viceroy. The term Khedive means 'great prince', 'man of authority', and though as a title it is less dignified than that of Sulṭán, it is more honourable than that of Viceroy. At the same time the Porte allowed the hereditary succession from father to son in the Khedival dynasty, but in return for the concession raised the annual tribute from £400,000 to £750,000. From time to time there has been friction between the two countries and Turkey, as suzerain, has tried to claim power and influence which could not be accorded or allowed to her.

In a fit of madness the Khedive 'Abbás Hílme, now in Constantinople, has thrown in his lot with Enver Bey and the Germans, and has therefore forfeited all right to his rule in Egypt, of which country he thus declares himself the enemy. The British Government at once declared Egypt a British Protectorate and has appointed Prince Ḥusain, an uncle of the late Khedive, as Sulṭán of Egypt under the suzerainty and the powerful protection of Great Britain. His Majesty King George V has sent him the following gracious and encouraging message :—

On the occasion of Your Highness entering on your high office, I desire to convey an expression of my most sincere friendship and an assurance of my unfailing support in safeguarding the integrity of Egypt and securing her future well-being and prosperity. Your Highness has been called upon to undertake the responsibilities of your high office at a grave crisis in the national life of Egypt.

I feel convinced that you will be able, with the co-operation of your Ministers and the protectorate of Great Britain, successfully to overcome all influences, which are seeking to destroy the independence of Egypt and the wealth, liberty and happiness of its people.

This important change in the relation of Egypt to Turkey has been well received by all classes of the Egyptian people. All connexion with Turkey now ceases, the Porte will have no further claim to the large annual tribute, and the Ottoman Sulṭáns will lose whatever dignity the office of suzerain of Egypt afforded them. Egypt will now be free to carry out many reforms, to the execution of which there have been many hindrances, and under its new Sulṭán will enter upon a period of real progress. The Germans have thus, though quite unwittingly, rendered a very real service to that wonderful land.

I have now traced the rise of a great empire from very small beginnings, and its gradual decline from a high position to its present almost hopeless condition. For a long while the Ottoman empire was a terror to south-eastern Europe; in more recent times it has been the despair of European statesmen. When its Sulṭáns led victorious armies and ravaged many lands, the empire maintained its military domination; when these Sulṭáns ceased to be leaders in warfare and spent their boyhood and early manhood in the secluded life of the harem they lost their virility and the empire became weak. As a conquering people the Ottomans showed some measure of imperial strength; when the tide of conquest turned and the state required men of broader sympathies and more liberal vision—statesmen in the best sense of the term—their incapacity was revealed. Called upon to rule over nations of many races and creeds they sadly failed; granted an entrance into the circle of civilized and progressive states, when administrative ability and a readiness to adapt themselves to a changing order of things was demanded, they have failed in a still greater degree.

Turkey has survived longer than the vigorous Khalífates of Damascus and of Baghdad, longer even than the brilliant Khalífate in Spain; but it has not been able to keep its position amongst the progressive nations of the West. They have long since passed away; and the causes which led to the decadence and disappearance of these once mighty Khalífates are working slowly, but with equal certainty towards the complete dissolution of the Ottoman empire. Muslim states seem to be able to reach a certain standard of greatness; but there is something in their law and polity which places an effective barrier to a continued rise in the scale of national progress in its highest forms, and to a lasting prosperity. The reason for this is not far to seek. It lies in their contemptuous disregard of all non-Muslim peoples, and in the rigid character of their sacred law. As expounded by its official interpreters that law is the most perfect the world has ever seen, and is therefore final. It thus becomes a great barrier to the highest development of a nation, which from its position in Europe is bound to hold intercourse and to have diplomatic, commercial and social relations with other nations, whose laws are more flexible and whose constitutions are progressive.

In these circumstances, a nation, dominated by laws and polity of this character, reaches a state which is like the association of sterility with vitality—the contact of the dead with the living. If Turkey is to have a future it must be in Asia and not in Europe, where it has for many years and in a multitude of ways proved a disastrous failure.

APPENDIX A

THE OTTOMAN SULTANS

NAME	DATE OF ACCESSION
ʻUthmán I	1299
Orkhan	1326
Murád I	1359
Báyazíd I	1389
Interregnum	
Muḥammad I	1402
Murád II	1421
Muḥammad II, the Conqueror	1451
Báyazíd II	1481
Salím I	1512
Suleymán I, the Magnificent	1520
Salím II	1566
Murád III	1574
Muḥammad III	1595
Aḥmad I	1603
Muṣṭafá I	1617
ʻUthmán II	1618
Murád IV	1623
Ibráhím	1640
Muḥammad IV	1648

NAME	DATE OF ACCESSION
Suleymán II	1687
Aḥmad II	1691
Muṣṭafá II	1695
Aḥmad III	1703
Maḥmúd I	1730
‘Uthmán III	1754
Muṣṭafá III	1757
‘Abdu’l-Ḥamíd I	1773
Salím III	1789
Muṣṭafá IV	1807
Maḥmúd II	1808
‘Abdu’l-Mejid	1839
‘Abdu’l-‘Azíz	1861
Murád V	1876
‘Abdu’l-Ḥamíd II	1876
Muḥammad V	1909

APPENDIX B

OTTOMAN SLAVERY AS AN IMPERIAL ASSET

THE practice of the 'Abbásid Khalífas, the Egyptian Mamlúk Sulṭáns, and the Muslim rulers in Spain followed the tendency of all oriental Governments, which rest on force, to rely on slaves brought from a distance or otherwise obtained. The Ottoman Sulṭáns developed this practice still further by levying a tribute of children from their Christian subjects, and thus they raised the whole system of slavery into an institution closely bound up with the military and civil administration of the empire, the prosperity of which was largely indebted to it. Sulṭán Muḥammad II, the Conqueror made this quite clear in these striking words: 'Our empire is the House of Islám, from father to son the lamp of our empire is kept bright with oil from the hearts of the infidels.'[1]

Some slaves were captives made in war; some were purchased or received as gifts; but the majority when mere lads were forcibly taken from Christian homes. This inhuman custom set aside the finer instincts of human nature, took no heed of parental affection,

[1] Quoted in Lyber, *Ottoman Empire in the time of Suleymán* (Harvard, 1912), p. 64.

disregarded the breaking up of family life, and ignored the rights of parents to bring up their children in their own law and religion. The lads thus taken were brought up as Muslims, and kept in the status of slaves and were under the absolute control of the Sulṭán.

This tribute of young boys was raised chiefly in the Balkans and in this manner. The country was divided into districts, and a capable official was appointed to travel about in each district with instructions to send to Constantinople a fixed number of the most vigorous and promising of the youths he could find. He required the priest of a village to furnish him with a list of baptized lads, between the ages of twelve and twenty, from whom he selected the sturdiest and handsomest ones until the required number was made up.

On arrival at Constantinople they were carefully trained for the military or the civil service. They were taught to look up to the Sulṭán as their lord, who could promote them to great honour and grant them posts of distinction, should they show by their devotion to him that they were worthy of such treatment. An Italian writer,[1] who in the reign of Suleymán II visited Constantinople, tells us that they were entertained in a large and spacious building under the charge of eunuchs, and richly clothed. In due course they were appointed by the Sulṭán spahi-oghlans (cavalry subalterns) or even to higher ranks in the army, or became Janissaries or Kapurjis (wardens of the gate).

[1] Probably Benedetto Ramberli whose work was published in Venice in 1545. See Lyber, *Ottoman Empire in the time of Suleymán*, Appendix I.

This careful system of education and the glittering prospects held out to them soon made the lads forget the homes of their childhood and inspired them with personal devotion to the Sulṭán, who often found in them his best servants and most valiant soldiers. By their conversion to Islám they became naturalized subjects of a new nation, and members of a fresh social and religious system. Separated entirely from the faith and traditions of their forefathers they became inspired with a new spirit and entered cheerfully upon a fresh life. This large annual addition to the ranks of Islám increased the wealth and power of the state. Thus 'the oil from the hearts of the infidel' kept the lamp of empire burning and the empire became possessed of an asset of great value.

If we set aside all moral considerations, there is no doubt that for many centuries the system by its provision of warriors and efficient administrators was a real source of strength. It is true that the time came when the military section became turbulent and had to be suppressed, but for many centuries the Ottoman empire owed much of its prestige and power to men of Christian birth thus alienated from their kith and kin. The pure Turk is not, as a rule, a good administrator and some of the ablest servants of the State were renegades, or of non-Ottoman origin. Enver Bey is not a wise statesman, but he is a vigorous, masterful man and he is of Polish extraction.

Suleymán II was one of the greatest men the Turks have produced. He knew his people, and how dim the lamp of empire would become, unless fed with oil from the heart of the infidel or, to drop the metaphor, how necessary it was, by some means or other, to strengthen the administration of the state by importing into its body politic men of a more virile character and of a more reliable disposition than the ordinary Turk. To gain and retain this valuable asset, the system of slavery which I have described became an important institution of the Ottoman empire.

APPENDIX C

OTTOMAN LITERATURE

THE Turks, at the outset of their career, were men of the sword rather than of the pen, and though they despised the Persians as a people less martial than themselves, they accepted entire their literary system and so based Ottoman literature upon a Persian model. A number of learned Ṣúfís had their home at Qonya, (Iconium) the capital of the Seljúks. The famous mystical poet, Jalálu'd-dín Rúmí, came there as a lad and soon became the most famous of them all. He is known throughout the East by his great work, the *Mathnaví*, on the form and style of which Ottoman poetry has been based. The style was simple, but in due time gave place to one in which 'curiosities of imagery gradually replaced the old straightforward speech'. Stanley Lane-Poole says: 'If we except the long narrative poems, the range of subjects sung by the muses of Persia and Turkey is very limited. Love, with its woes and joys, naturally and by right assumes the first place; then we have the charms of the spring-tide, the sweet song of the nightingale, the beauty of the flowers, and other delightful things of Nature, generally with the undertone of religious mysticism throughout. And that is well nigh all.'[1]

[1] *Turkey*, p. 302.

The Ottoman poets of the early period showed no originality but simply copied and followed all they could find of excellence in the poetry of the Persians: 'The prose in its higher flights is generally bombastic, often involved, and like the poetry, bristles with equivoques and other verbal tricks, which though frequently ingenious, are more or less trivial and always give a forced and unnatural appearance to the style.'[1] In the reign of Sulṭán Suleymán (1520–66) two poets, Fuzúlí and Báki, arose and introduced a new era. Fuzúlí was a writer of eminence. He still conforms to the Persian style, but is more original than any of his predecessors. Fifty years later Náfí of Erzerúm elaborated a style for himself, but being a satirist and having the imprudence to exercise his wit on men of influence he was executed by the order of Sulṭán Murád IV. In each succeeding age authors in prose and poetry arose, some of whom were eminent, but the literature as a whole still remained under the domination of the Persian influence.

A change, however, has now come over it. It began in 1859 with a translation of some French poetry into Turkish, thus showing that good literature was to be found outside the world of Islám. In 1879 'Abdu'l-Ḥaqq Aḥmad Beg published some poems in a simple style and according to Western forms. Others followed and a revolt from the long-established influence of Persian poetry commenced. 'Some thirty years ago a wonderful change began to come over Turkish literature, and this change has ever since been growing yearly

[1] S. Lane-Poole, *Turkey*, p. 303.

more and more marked, altering the whole tone and spirit, as well as the external form of Ottoman literary work. . . . The change is a result of the study of the French language and literature which has become general only within the last twenty years. Marvellous, indeed, have been its effects. In poetry likewise Western forms have well-nigh superseded the monorhythmic g͟hazals and qaṣidas of the olden time. Of course all these changes have not been effected without opposition; many Turks of the old school, admirers of the Persian style and haters of all things Western, opposed them bitterly, and some oppose them still; but the battle has virtually been fought, the victory won, and for good or ill Europe has conquered Asia, Paris has replaced Shíráz.' [1]

The new learning, full of western thought and ideas, has been an important factor in the formation of the Young Turkey Party. One of the best informed European students of Turkish literature, the late E. J. W. Gibb, saw clearly how its improvement would affect the whole position of affairs. He says: 'This period of twenty years (1859–79) is thus the turning-point in the evolution of the new civilization of Turkey; all that had gone before since the days of the martyred Salím has been leading up to the revolution now accomplished; what follows is its development.' [2] The repressive measures of the late Turkish Government sent into exile men whose mental horizon had thus widened, but the leaven was at work, the intellectual condition of the best men

[1] S. Lane-Poole, *Turkey*, pp. 322-3.

[2] *History of Ottoman Poetry* (1907), vol. v, pp. 18-20.

was being profoundly changed, a high sense of duty was being created and a true patriotism was being formed. The exiles from amongst the literary men had to be joined during the last twenty years by men from the various professions, and some nobles, exiled by the jealousy and the fear of the palace clique, before any practical steps were taken to set aside the despotism of ʻAbdu'l-Ḥamíd ; but it must never be forgotten that the movement towards reform, which it was hoped the Young Turkey Party would bring about, owes not a little of its force to those learned authors, who in modern days have reconstructed the literature, widened its boundaries, and brought it into living contact with the West. Thus it seemed as if the 'new learning' would become a powerful force in the social emancipation, in the religious freedom, and in the political elevation of the Turkey of to-day. All these hopes and aspirations, however, have not been realized, for the Young Turks by their arrogant militarism have not only retarded the reform movement, but seem likely to bring about the ruin of the empire.

INDEX

Works by the same Author

The Faith of Islam (S.P.C.K., London and Madras. 5*s.* Rs. 4.)

'A scholarly exposition and epitome of the various tenets embraced by Islám. Nothing but praise can be said of the whole undertaking.' *RASJ*, October, 1897.

'The importance of a book of this kind is very great.' Stanley Lane-Poole in the *Academy*.

'This volume gives us more information about the doctrines and polity of Islám than any book of moderate size with which we are acquainted.' *Spectator.*

The Historical Development of the Qur'an (S.P.C.K., London and Madras. 3*s.* Rs. 2.)

'In Mr. Sell's hands the Qur'án becomes a new book and sheds a flood of light on the character of its author, and the movement he initiated and guided.' Marcus Dods in the *Critical Review.*

Islam: its rise and progress (Simpkin Marshall & Co., London; S.P.C.K., Madras. 9*d.* As. 9.)

The Religious Orders of Islam (Simpkin Marshall & Co., London; S.P.C.K., Madras. 1*s.* As. 12.)

Also the following volumes of the ISLAM SERIES published by the Christian Literature Society.

The Cult of 'Ali.
The Druses.
Sufiism.
Ghazwas and Sariyas.
The Battles of Badr and of Uhud.
Bahaism.
Al-Qur'an.
The Recensions of the Qur'an.
The Hanifs.
Outlines of Islam.
Islam in China.
The Four Rightly-Guided Khalifas.
The Umayyad and 'Abbasid Khalifates.
Muslim Conquests in North Africa.
The Mamluks in Egypt.
Muslim Conquests in Spain.
The Ottoman Turks.

La Conquete du Monde Musulman (Paris, 1912) speaks of the Islám Series as 'Manuels destinés à vulgariser la counaissance de la religion, de l'histoíre et de la vie Musulmanes,' and as a 'véritable petite encyclopédie mi-didactic, mi-polémique.'